Simulating Information Retrieval Test Collections

Synthesis Lectures on Information Concepts, Retrieval, and Services

Editor
Gary Marchionini, *University of North Carolina, Chapel Hill*

Synthesis Lectures on Information Concepts, Retrieval, and Services publishes short books on topics pertaining to information science and applications of technology to information discovery, production, distribution, and management. Potential topics include: data models, indexing theory and algorithms, classification, information architecture, information economics, privacy and identity, scholarly communication, bibliometrics and webometrics, personal information management, human information behavior, digital libraries, archives and preservation, cultural informatics, information retrieval evaluation, data fusion, relevance feedback, recommendation systems, question answering, natural language processing for retrieval, text summarization, multimedia retrieval, multilingual retrieval, and exploratory search.

Simulating Information Retrieval Test Collections

David Hawking, Bodo Billerbeck, Paul Thomas, and Nick Craswell

ISBN: 978-3-031-01195-5   paperback
ISBN: 978-3-031-02323-1   ebook
ISBN: 978-3-031-00230-4   hardcover

DOI 10.1007/978-3-031-02323-1

A Publication in the Springer series
SYNTHESIS LECTURES ON INFORMATION CONCEPTS, RETRIEVAL, AND SERVICES

Lecture #71
Series Editor: Gary Marchionini, *University of North Carolina, Chapel Hill*
Series ISSN
Print 1947-945X   Electronic 1947-9468

Simulating Information Retrieval Test Collections

David Hawking
Australian National University, Canberra

Bodo Billerbeck
Microsoft Bing

Paul Thomas
Microsoft Bing

Nick Craswell
Microsoft Bing

SYNTHESIS LECTURES ON INFORMATION CONCEPTS, RETRIEVAL, AND SERVICES #71

ABSTRACT

Simulated test collections may find application in situations where real datasets cannot easily be accessed due to confidentiality concerns or practical inconvenience. They can potentially support Information Retrieval (IR) experimentation, tuning, validation, performance prediction, and hardware sizing. Naturally, the accuracy and usefulness of results obtained from a simulation depend upon the fidelity and generality of the models which underpin it. The fidelity of emulation of a real corpus is likely to be limited by the requirement that confidential information in the real corpus should not be able to be extracted from the emulated version. We present a range of methods exploring trade-offs between emulation fidelity and degree of preservation of privacy.

We present three different simple types of text generator which work at a micro level: Markov models, neural net models, and substitution ciphers. We also describe macro level methods where we can engineer macro properties of a corpus, giving a range of models for each of the salient properties: document length distribution, word frequency distribution (for independent and non-independent cases), word length and textual representation, and corpus growth.

We present results of emulating existing corpora and for scaling up corpora by two orders of magnitude. We show that simulated collections generated with relatively simple methods are suitable for some purposes and can be generated very quickly. Indeed it may sometimes be feasible to embed a simple lightweight corpus generator into an indexer for the purpose of efficiency studies.

Naturally, a corpus of artificial text cannot support IR experimentation in the absence of a set of compatible queries. We discuss and experiment with published methods for query generation and query log emulation.

We present a proof-of-the-pudding study in which we observe the predictive accuracy of efficiency and effectiveness results obtained on emulated versions of TREC corpora. The study includes three open-source retrieval systems and several TREC datasets. There is a trade-off between confidentiality and prediction accuracy and there are interesting interactions between retrieval systems and datasets. Our tentative conclusion is that there are emulation methods which achieve useful prediction accuracy while providing a level of confidentiality adequate for many applications.

Many of the methods described here have been implemented in the open source project SynthaCorpus, accessible at:

> https://bitbucket.org/davidhawking/synthacorpus/

KEYWORDS

information retrieval, simulated test collections, text generation, modeling, natural language generation

Contents

Acknowledgments

We gratefully acknowledge: Jan Pedersen, Katja Hoffman, and Walter Sun for their useful suggestions on modeling; Tom Minka for gamma fitting code; Andrew Trotman, Fernando Diaz, and Craig Macdonald, for assistance with ATIRE, Indri, and Terrier search engines, respectively; Bhaskar Mitra and Nick Lester for pointers and valuable discussions; and Jacques Savoy for advice on stylistic analysis of text.

David Hawking, Bodo Billerbeck, Paul Thomas, and Nick Craswell
August 2020

Symbols

$\mathbb{B}$	Base: A real-world document corpus, e.g. TREC-AP
$\mathbb{M}$	Mimic: An emulated document corpus
$\mathbb{S}$	A scaled-up document corpus
$\mathbb{A}$	An alphabet
N	The number of documents in a corpus
P	The total number of word occurrences (postings) in a corpus
f	The total number of occurrences of a word in a corpus
tf	The number of occurrences of a word in a particular document
df	The number of documents in which a word occurs
$|V|$	The size of a vocabulary
w_1	The proportion of distinct words which occur only once
h	The number of head points explicitly modeled in the piecewise model of a word frequency distribution
$H_1 \ldots H_h$	The percentages of all word occurrences represented by each of the most frequent h words ($h > 0$)
s	The number of piecewise segments used to model the middle section of a word frequency distribution ($s > 0$)
$S_1 \ldots S_s$	The 4-tuples of the s segments
R_1	Prediction accuracy ratio. Ratio of smaller to larger measurement
R_2	Ratio of a measurement to a reference measurement
KLD	Kullback–Leibler divergence between two probability distributions
JSD	Jensen–Shannon divergence between two probability distributions
BD	Bhattacharyya distance between two probability distributions
KSS	Kolmogorov–Smirnov distance between two probability distributions

CHAPTER 1

Introduction

Test collections provide a foundation for the academic field of information retrieval (IR). They provide a vital means by which retrieval algorithms can be compared and tuned. Over the decades, empirical work on test collections has led to important theoretical insights.

A test collection generally comprises three components: a fixed corpus of documents (the units of retrieval); a set of statements of information need (sometimes in the form of queries); and a set of relevance judgments identifying the documents which are most useful in satisfying each of the information needs.

The most influential creator of test collections and promoter of research using them is the United States National Institute of Standards and Technology (NIST) through the Text Retrieval Conference (TREC) [87].[1] TREC has created test collections for several different languages, and for different types of document. TREC collections have modeled different types of information need, and different types of user.

Most test collection research has aimed to improve the ability of a retrieval system to retrieve useful documents ahead of less useful ones. This is known as the *effectiveness* of a retrieval system. Many different measures of effectiveness have been used, including mean average precision (MAP) [87, p. 59] and normalized discounted cumulative gain (NDCG) [51]. Sanderson 2010 [77] presents an extensive review of IR evaluation based on test collections.

In addition to supporting study of retrieval effectiveness, test collections have been the main resource for researchers studying the *efficiency* of retrieval systems—How fast can document corpora be indexed? How quickly can indexes be updated to respond to additions and deletions of content? How fast can queries be processed? How much benefit can be gained by caching results for popular queries? How much overhead is incurred by enforcing document-level access controls? What retrieval architectures are best for retrieval over extremely large corpora? What are the trade-offs between speed of retrieval and retrieval effectiveness?

Both efficiency and effectiveness of retrieval are of great importance to industry. Efficiency gains can sometimes result in millions of dollars in savings, and effectiveness is critical to delivering value to customers and users. Unfortunately, search companies must often work with retrieval scenarios which are not well modeled by public test collections. For example, a retrieval system tuned on TREC Ad Hoc retrieval tasks may not perform well in responding to an individual's searches over their personal email archive.

---

[1]http://trec.nist.gov

A search company may need to build its own test collections to tune effectiveness and to size the hardware needed to support an effective and responsive search service. Unfortunately, due to confidentiality concerns, the search company may not be allowed to access either the actual documents held by a customer, or user queries and interactions. This is one motivation for simulating test collections. We discuss this and others in the next section.

1.1   MOTIVATIONS FOR SIMULATED TEST COLLECTIONS

There are a number of real-world applications in which it is useful to generate an artificial text corpus with a corresponding set of test queries. A prime example is when a cloud hosting company (like Microsoft) builds search systems for hosted clients whose data is confidential. The hosting company wishes to measure and improve indexing performance and query processing latency and throughput, to tune a ranking function, and to experiment with auxiliary features such as query suggestion and spelling correction, *without its employees having access to client documents or queries*. If confidentiality constraints allow an automated agent to extract sufficient properties of a client's data then the hosting company can build a simulated collection and work with it.

An example of the real-world use of simulated text corpora occurred within Microsoft a few years ago. It had been tentatively decided to replace one indexing and querying system within the email service Exchange 365 with another. Would the new system be able to operate on the hardware resources currently allocated, and would it be able to achieve the required latencies and throughput? The answers to these questions were of critical importance, since there were hundreds of millions of mailboxes to migrate.

For academic research, simulated corpora can permit exact reproducibility of efficiency experiments and meaningful study of the scalability of retrieval systems. A corpus can potentially be shared exactly with other researchers by communicating a few kilobytes of parameters, while completely eliminating confounds due to differences in tokenization and other lexical issues. Furthermore, a parameterized collection generator allows data sets to be engineered to specification, permitting focused study of specific efficiency or effectiveness factors. Finally, a comprehensive generative model also models the growth of a corpus, allowing retrieval systems to be tested on data sets as they might become in the future.

We discuss the challenge of creating simulated test collections capable of supporting the tuning of ranking functions and other IR services, *while maintaining confidentiality of the information in the real collection*, and present some preliminary results.

1.2   PAST WORK ON SIMULATION IN IR

There is a long history of simulation in the field of IR. Our overview of the literature focuses on simulation of offline test collections, but we also give some examples of other uses of simulation in IR.

The first system we know of for generating artificial documents is due to Michael Cooper [25]. Cooper's system first created an artificial block of text by generating words according to an observed word frequency distribution and assigning them to simulated word classes. It then created a thesaurus by examining word associations in the simulated text. The thesaurus was used in the process of generating both pseudo-documents and pseudo-queries. A pseudo-document consisted of reduced representations such as an abstract and index terms. For each representation, a random length was calculated, some starter words were generated and then additional related words were drawn from the thesaurus. As can be appreciated, the simulation model was quite sophisticated but the work was severely limited by the computer hardware of the time. Experiments used a 200 word vocabulary, 150 documents, and a maximum of 20 words per document representation.

A 1978 Ph.D. thesis by Griffiths [40] extended the work of Cooper to generate simulated queries and to simulate relevance judgments. Unfortunately, we have been unable to access this thesis and rely on a brief description of it by Gordon in 1990 [39, p. 314].

Gordon himself inverts the normal retrieval evaluation model. Given the set of relevant (query, document) pairs, the usual approach is to evaluate how many relevant documents are retrieved by a system for a sample of queries. He argues that it is equivalent to start with a sample of documents and look at the proportion of *relevant queries* for which they are retrieved. Taking this approach, he used humans to generate short descriptions of each of a set of sampled documents. He treated those as relevant queries for the documents. He also suggested the use of alternative automated methods such as relevance feedback to develop the set of relevant queries. In order to assess the performance of a retrieval method, he used a set of *nonrelevant queries* to measure fallout, the proportion of nonrelevant queries for which the document is retrieved. His nonrelevant set was made up of queries which were similar to the relevant ones. He claimed that retrieval methods could be simulated and compared, without access to an IR system, using this approach.

In 1980, Tague et al. [84] described a system for generating a document-term matrix using a Poisson distribution for document lengths and Zipf-like term generation. Tague et al. reviewed a number of multivariate probability functions for the distribution of index terms over documents, including a model of term dependence due to van Rijsbergen [85]. Again due to the limitations of the era, empirical validation was limited to very small data sets.

In a precursor to our own work, Zobel et al. [95] created a simulated test collection in order to compare document signatures and inverted files as alternative methods of text indexing.

Their corpus generator FINNEGAN built a language model from a large number of books then available on the Internet. The authors claimed that FINNEGAN generated text with similar statistical properties to real text. Document lengths were modeled using a gamma distribution. Their query generator QUANGLE generated queries from the vocabulary of the corpus, after excluding various stop and other non-content words. Given a number q of conjuncts, a number m of disjuncts per conjunct and a desired number A of answers it generated Boolean queries in conjunctive normal form.

Baeza-Yates and Navarro [6] present models for many aspects of document corpora, including word frequencies, word lengths, document lengths, the relationship between the size of a corpus and it's vocabulary, the properties of query streams, and the size of retrieval answer sets. They do not, however, use their models for the purposes of simulation.

In 2005, Webber and Moffat [89] pointed out the many difficulties in carrying out reliable retrieval experiments, particularly in the context of large-scale distributed methods. They described a method for converting an available query log related to one corpus into a simulated log for another corpus for which no significant log was available. They addressed the challenge of how to make the simulated log relate to the second corpus in a realistic way.

Azzopardi, de Rijke and Balog, e.g. [3] and [4], have presented and evaluated methods for generating known-item queries from document corpora. We review other methods for the generation of simulated query sets in Chapter 8.

Our work addresses only the problem of generating artificial offline test collections for information retrieval experimentation and tuning, but for the interest of readers we now briefly mention some other uses of simulation in information retrieval.

1.2.1 OTHER APPLICATIONS OF SIMULATION IN IR

In 1966, Blunt et al. [14] wrote a report for the U.S. Office of Naval Research, proposing a general simulation model of an entire information retrieval system, including personnel and equipment, with the aim of being able to eliminate delays and bottlenecks in the retrieval of important information. In 1968, Baker and Nance [7] presented an even broader simulation including funders of information storage and retrieval systems. These papers are representative of quite a number of simulation studies from the 1960s in an era where the possibilities of automated information storage and retrieval were only just emerging, and where the cost and latency of retrieving information were significant factors, e.g.: Bourne and Ford [16], Hayes and Reilly [44], Reilly [70, 71], and Fried [37].

Heine [46] presents an overview of simulation in information retrieval, discussing the variety of definitions of key terms such as "simulation," "model," and "system." He outlines eight different systems relating to information retrieval which might be studied using simulation, gives three example scenarios, and reviews simulation work up to the time of his writing.

A number of papers have used simulation models to compare and evaluate distributed information retrieval architectures, without generating artificial test collections. For example, Cacheda et al. [17] and Cahoon and McKinley [18].

Kanungo [52] describes a system for generating artificial corpora of degraded text, suitable for experimentation with OCR systems. He also describes a method for validating degradation models. Croft et al. [28] also work with simulated OCR data.

Kim and Croft [53] built a simulated collection of documents suitable for desktop search by taking W3C emails distributed as part of the TREC Enterprise Track and gathering from the web documents relating to people mentioned in the emails.

Robertson et al. [75] report the use of simulated relevance scores in investigating score-distributional ideas.

There has been a lot of relatively recent work on simulating user interactions with information retrieval systems, such as: Azzopardi [2], Maxwell [62], Foley and Smeaton [35]; Borlund and Schneider [15], and Chi et al. [22].

Simulation is clearly a well-established research method in the field of information retrieval.

1.3   OUR WORK ON SIMULATION

In this work we report a quite thorough study of many aspects of the collection simulation problem. We study the properties of a range of different corpora and discuss alternative generative models.

We have developed a set of open source tools (SYNTHACORPUS[2]) for extracting properties from an existing corpus and for generating parameterized corpora using multiple alternative models. We compare the properties of corpora emulated using SYNTHACORPUS tools with those of the corresponding originals.

We don't claim that the tools in SYNTHACORPUS are complete or perfect. Indeed, there are many opportunities for capability extensions and code improvements. We hope that readers will take the opportunity to contribute to the open source project and that contributed extensions will permit even more faithful test collection simulations.

In order to build models of corpus growth for implementation in SYNTHACORPUS we studied samples of the corpora and plotted changes in properties as the samples grow from 1% to 100% of the parent. Then, starting with a static model of the smallest sample and modifying it according to a growth model, we generated a corpus 100 times larger. We show that its properties are quite similar to the original. Note that the growth in vocabulary as corpus size increases, as described by Herdan and Heaps [34, 45, 48], prevents us from using the original corpus vocabulary when scaling up, even when the original data is public.

In order to permit the study of query processing efficiency and effectiveness over artificially generated corpora, SYNTHACORPUS implements a version of Azzopardi et al.'s best-performing method for generating known-item queries. We use it extensively in our experiments. SYNTHA-CORPUS also provides a facility similar to that of Webber and Moffat for converting a real query

[2]https://bitbucket.org/davidhawking/synthacorpus/

```
Soos of chos of joint perfomine the wonse in the 192: Minion.
Incoughavatems, by at there Ileappption.The mediff DELED.
```

Figure 1.1: Example text generated by a DMC compression model. Reproduced from Bell et al. [8].

log corresponding to a real corpus, into an emulated query log for an emulated version of the real corpus.

It is not exactly known which properties of a corpus have the greatest influence on efficiency, resource requirements, and effectiveness of a retrieval system. Indeed, the relative importance of the properties likely depends on both the algorithm and the characteristics of the hardware architecture. A thorough study of these dependencies is beyond the scope of the present work, but we empirically compare the ability of a number of different simulation methods to predict results on a real corpus, for three different open source IR systems.

A real corpus can be emulated with different degrees of fidelity. It may be impractical to faithfully emulate a corpus either due to the cost of generation or due to potential leakage of confidential information. Our study sheds light on the range of degrees of fidelity and the costs of achieving a specified level.

In the next few sections we paint a broad picture of the range of methods which can be used for generating artificial text.

1.4   TEXT GENERATION; TEXT COMPRESSION

We start by briefly mentioning the relationship between text generation and text compression.

Text compression schemes rely on models of the text being compressed—the more accurate the model, the greater the compression which may be achieved. Bell et al. [8, p. 256] show that models used for compressing text can also be used to generate synthetic text. They give examples of synthetic text generated by models learned by different compression schemes. Figure 1.1 quotes a section of one such example.

Text compression methods, like text generation methods, use a range of different text models. However, the goal of text compression is to achieve a highly compact representation of the text from which the original can be perfectly reconstructed. Text generation does not aim for compactness and, when confidentiality of information is a concern, should not allow reconstruction of the original.

Plain Text: Round the rugged rocks the ragged rascal ran.

Relevant part of nomenclator table:
```
round  → Smith
ragged → twice
ran    → and
rascal → Tuesday
rocks  → B52
rugged → it
the    → furlong
```

Ciphertext: Smith furlong it B52 furlong twice Tuesday and

Figure 1.2: Illustration of the Nomenclator method.

1.5   METHODS IMPLEMENTED IN SYNTHACORPUS

1.5.1   TEXT GENERATION AS ENCRYPTION

Possibly the simplest method for emulating a base corpus $\mathbb{B}$ is to encrypt it using a substitution cipher. Many substitution ciphers are described in the Wikipedia article https://en.wikipedia.org/wiki/Substitution_cipher. Potentially, encryption of a corpus could provide a degree of protection of confidential information.

Simple letter substitution ciphers are easily cracked using letter frequency information and hence provide no effective protection of confidential information. SYNTHACORPUS provides an implementation of the Caesar cipher, in which each letter is replaced by a letter a fixed distance away in the alphabet, with wrap-around.[3] The Caesar method is only used here as an [unrealistic] baseline.

Substitution of letter digrams or trigrams results in stronger encryption, but once the substitutions are known, even very rare words can be decrypted. The Wikipedia article referenced above also discusses a substitution scheme which potentially provides much more protection. It is the so-called Nomenclator cipher, used from the 15th century in the French royal court. It defines substitution rules for words, syllables, and letters. When the substitution table is large, plain text encrypted in this way is very hard to decrypt.

SYNTHACORPUS implements a simplified version of Nomenclator, using only word-for-word substitutions. Each word in $\mathbb{B}$ is replaced by the corresponding word in a parallel vocabulary. The parallel vocabulary can be a permutation of the original, a vocabulary of equal or greater size from a different corpus, or a list of made-up words. This form of encryption requires a large mapping table between the vocabularies, but can be very fast. Figure 1.2 illustrates the method.

---

[3]Note that this implementation translates only the ASCII letters.

On the downside, the method is constrained to emulation of an original corpus. It is not feasible to create a scaled-up emulation of $\mathbb{B}$,[4] nor to create a range of corpora with similar properties to $\mathbb{B}$, nor to engineer a corpus to have specified properties.

We want to be able to generate corpora in all those scenarios, but the use case addressed by Nomenclator is an important one. We present results for the NOMENCLATOR algorithm (and also CAESAR) in Chapter 9.

NOMENCLATOR does a much better job than CAESAR of preserving confidentiality. See Chapter 11, page 142, for a discussion of this.

Both CAESAR and NOMENCLATOR methods have some very useful emulation properties.

1. Distributions of word frequency, n-gram frequency, and document length are identical to the originals.

2. Albeit with increased risk to confidentiality, document mark-up and inter document link structure can be preserved, along with punctuation and metadata.

3. Query logs including clicks can be used in emulation experiments because the same encryption scheme can be applied to queries as well as documents.

Example TREC-AP fragments emulated with CAESAR1 (top) and NOMENCLATOR (bottom) are shown in Figure 1.3

1.5.2   SIMPLE LANGUAGE MODELS FOR TEXT GENERATION

Generative language models used in IR are typically used to assess the likelihood that a document and a query were generated from the same model, rather than to actually generate text. They could, however, be used for synthetic corpus generation, as illustrated in the following BASE-LINE algorithm, which is very similar to the method implemented by Zobel et al.'s FINNEGAN program [95]. It is also very similar to the WBMARKOV0 method introduced in Section 3.1, differing only in the manner of determining document lengths.

1. Extract a unigram language model (LM) from a base corpus $\mathbb{B}$, representing the language model as a cumulative probability histogram.

2. Repeat the following until the desired amount of text has been generated:

   (a) Generate a pseudo-random document length l (in words) from a length distribution derived from $\mathbb{B}$.

   (b) Generate l uniformly distributed random numbers in the range $0 \ldots 1$. Use the cumulative probability histogram to map each of them to a word and emit that word.

   (c) Emit a document boundary marker.

---

[4]For example, an emulation of $\mathbb{B}$ as it might become after substantial growth.

```
<DOC>
<DOCNO> CAESR1-000000 </DOCNO>
<TEXT>
Sfqpsut Gpsnfs Tbjhpo Pggjdjbmt Sfmfbtfe gspn Sf fevdbujpo Dbnq Npsf
uibo 261 gpsnfs pggjdfst pg uif pwfsuispxo Tpvui Wjfuobnftf hpwfsonfou
ibwf cffo sfmfbtfe gspn b sf fevdbujpo dbnq bgufs 24 zfbst pg
efufoujpo uif pggjdjbm Wjfuobn Ofxt Bhfodz sfqpsufe Tbuvsebz Uif
sfqpsu gspn Ibopj npojupsfe jo Cbohlpl eje opu hjwf tqfdjgjd gjhvsft
...
</TEXT>
</DOC>




<DOC>
<DOCNO> Nomen-0 </DOCNO>
<TEXT>
moschorsholt biarrithem vladish esbuscovar ngau competanya padrnos
kumsisant fu derauding abori cristyn bederick vladish chalis gierkeg
herbed bullistoforceab casperimentativ estheticaly nhilunbuy carlatt
bonnoticeable competanya padrnos acri kumsisant fu derauding juicines
recurragchaa scaffold gierkeg guntumbley herbed destructuring sepate
...
```

Figure 1.3: Examples of cipher-generated text. CAESAR1, (top) and NOMENCLATOR (bottom). The output vocabulary in the Nomenclator case is Markov generated.

We present the BASELINE algorithm to illustrate the general idea of corpus emulation, and also to illustrate the shortcomings of such a straightforward approach. Ideally, the resulting "mimic" corpus M should closely match the modeled properties of the original corpus but BASELINE suffers from a number of limitations.

1. Because we are sampling "with replacement"[5] the expected vocabulary size of M will be less than that of B since some words will likely not be sampled. We sometimes refer to this as *vocabulary shrinkage*. It is an issue with many of the text generation methods we discuss.

2. Words are generated independently. Phrase and sentence structure are not modeled and nor is the tendency of word occurences to cluster in documents.

---

[5]Sampling with and without replacement are standard statistical processes, defined in any good statistics text. When sampling with replacement, the probability of choosing a word remains constant regardless of how many times it has already been chosen. A word which occurred only once in B may occur multiple times in M or not at all.

3. The vocabulary of the synthetic corpus cannot be larger than that of the emulated one. Words not found in the base corpus cannot be emitted. That means that scaling $\mathbb{M}$ beyond the size of $\mathbb{B}$ will result in decreasing fidelity since laws due to Herdan [48] and Heaps [45] tell us that the vocabulary size of a real corpus should grow with the size of the text. Williams and Zobel [90] have confirmed this growth in much larger datasets than available to earlier authors.

We will see later on how to overcome these limitations.

Note that the size of a language model (probability histogram) may be large. A very large corpus may contain hundreds of millions of distinct words.

Despite its limitations, we present some experimental results for BASELINE. Naturally, the range of applications for a synthetic corpus can be increased if more sophisticated modeling is undertaken. A number of more sophisticated generative models are available.

1.5.3   MARKOV MODELS

The very simple language model described in the previous section can be considered to represent a Markov model of order zero, where the symbols are the words of the vocabulary. If an additional End-of-document (EOD) symbol is added to the vocabulary, a document-length distribution will arise naturally from the Markov generation process.

In a Markov model of order k, the probability of emitting a particular symbol depends on the k preceding symbols. An order zero model takes no account of context—the probability of emitting the word "aardvark" is independent of any of the words preceding it.

Higher-order Markov models could likely produce much more realistic text but the size of the models increases rapidly with their order. In a naïve (dense) implementation, an order one model (taking into account the word before the present one) would require storage of $|V|^2$ probabilities. Given that the vocabulary size of WT10g is at least 5 million, that implies 25 trillion probabilities!

Sparse methods dramatically reduce space requirements. The MARKOVGENERATOR program included in SYNTHACORPUS supports generation according to either order zero WB-MARKOV0 or order one WBMARKOV1 models. In the latter case the generator stores vocabulary words in a hash table whose entries reference a data structure for recording successor words and their frequencies. The choice of the data structure is critical to achieving reasonable speed. For each common word, successor words are stored in a subsidiary hash table. Once the scan of the training corpus is complete, the entries in the subsidiary hash are converted into an array of cumulative probabilities to enable efficient binary search during the generation phase. Successors of uncommon words are stored in linked lists.

Note that emulating $\mathbb{B}$ using a word-based Markov model trained on $\mathbb{B}$ will under-generate $\mathbb{B}$'s vocabulary, because we are effectively sampling with replacement.

One can overcome the limited vocabulary problem by training a high-order character-based Markov model. Another SYNTHACORPUS program STRINGMARKOVGEN works with an alphabet of letters rather than words but supports much higher orders. This allows for more natural modeling of word sequences and linguistic structures. Because the alphabet consists of letters rather than words, addition of a small amount of noise can be used to generate words which have not been seen in the training text and thus overcome the problem of vocabulary under-generation.

The addition of noise in STRINGMARKOVGEN is controlled by the parameters k, λ, and w. Noise is introduced by randomly, with probability λ, by generating the next symbol from a lower-order model. The order of the reduced model is $k - w$. Rather than maintaining a full transition matrix of order $k - w$, wild-carded versions of contexts (with w leading wildcards) are stored in the main transition matrix. To illustrate, let us assume that the order k of the model is 5, and that the value of w is 3. Say we encounter the sequence `genera` in the training data, i.e., we have a context string of `gener` and a successor character of a. We update the transition matrix to increment the count for a following `gener`. We then modify the context string by replacing the first w characters with the wildcard symbol * and increment the count for a following `***er`. We also update counts for a in contexts with $w + 1, \ldots, k$ wildcards.

Generating a symbol from a reduced context may result in a sequence of k characters which was never seen in training. Looking up that string will result in failure, requiring a fallback to the wildcarded version with w wildcards. That lookup may also fail, requiring fallback to the wildcarded version with $w + 1$ wildcards, and so on. The process is eventually guaranteed to succeed because lookup of the all-wildcard context cannot fail.

The choice of w comes down to a tradeoff between plausibility and efficiency. A low value of w results in more plausible text but increases the size of the transition matrix, and multiplies the number of additions to it by a factor of $k - w + 1$.

Experimental results are reported in later chapters for WBMARKOV0, WBMARKOV1, and STRINGMARKOV methods.

1.5.4   EMULATION TO ACHIEVE MACRO PROPERTIES

When used to generate a corpus, the language models described so far may be regarded as bottom-up methods. At each point the next word to be emitted depends upon an array or matrix of probabilities, accessed by a limited context of what has been generated so far. When emulating a base corpus $\mathbb{B}$ it is unlikely that the macro properties of $\mathbb{M}$ will closely match those of $\mathbb{B}$.

An alternative approach, implemented by the CORPUSGENERATOR tool provided in SYN-THACORPUS is to attempt to generate a corpus with specified macro properties. Specifically, CORPUSGENERATOR provides the ability to generate a corpus with the following characteristics:

1. Number of documents N.

2. Document length distribution.

3. Total number of word occurrences (postings) P. This is the main determinant of the scale of an indexing task.

4. Vocabulary size $|V|$. This determines the size of the word dictionary and influences the time taken by word insertions and lookups.

5. Word probability distribution. This determines the distribution of postings list lengths and the length of the longest postings list. The best choice of index data structures and algorithms may depend upon this.

6. Word dependence. We try to capture the tendency of certain pairs of words to associate within documents, the tendency of certain words to appear more often in particular documents than would be expected by chance, and the tendency of certain word n-grams to appear more often than would be expected by chance. At the time of writing, CORPUS-GENERATOR is able to model n-grams only. However, we present algorithms for modeling word burstiness and word co-occurrence.

7. Characteristics of word representations. The length of words and the patterns of characters in the representation may affect hash table collision rates or the efficiency of tree structures.

8. The tendency of short words to occur more frequently than long ones. (See Zipf [92].)

Generation controlled by specified macro properties allows the engineering of corpora with particular characteristics needed for experiments. When emulation of $\mathbb{B}$ is required, SYN-THACORPUS provides the CORPUSPROPERTYEXTRACTOR tool to determine parameters for the generator. The fidelity of emulation can be controlled by choosing more or less realistic models of the various properties. For example, one can emulate the document length distribution of a corpus by specifying a full table of the actual lengths, by specifying just the average length, or by giving the parameters of a mathematical distribution such as left-truncated normal, or gamma.

Depending upon the sophistication of the model to be used during generation the set of parameters to CORPUSGENERATOR may be very compact.

1.6   OTHER TEXT GENERATION MODELS

1.6.1   TOPIC MODELING VIA LATENT DIRICHLET ALLOCATION (LDA)

Approaches like LDA can be used to better model the tendency of subject words to cluster [13]. Separate language models are generated for topics represented in a corpus and documents are generated as a mixture of a subset of topics. For instance, Wallach et al. [88] propose a method to generate held-out documents given the remainder of a collection.

Despite the possibility of achieving greater realism in modeling, the LDA approach seems to entail a number of practical disadvantages: it is very likely to result in vocabulary under-generation; it is more challenging to train topic models than simple language models; like language models it requires large parameter sets; it has the potential to increase the risk of information leakage; and scaling up a corpus seems to require the ability to model future topics.

We have not experimented with LDA models.

1.6.2   *n*-GRAM LANGUAGE MODELS

In Section 1.5.3 we stated that simple language models were effectively Markov models of order zero, and that higher-order Markov models could be used to generate more natural sequences of words.

An alternative way of extending a simple language model (order zero Markov) would be to enhance the "alphabet" to include not only single words but *n*-grams,[6] such as named entities. Each such *n*-gram, e.g., "President Obama" or "probabilistic ranking principle," would be associated with a probability of occurrence. The probabilities of all terms, whether single words or *n*-grams, would sum to one.

Chen and Goodman [21] experiment with language models comprising only 2-grams or only 3-grams. They identify the critical importance of smoothing to enable appropriate treatment of word strings not seen in the training data. The focus of their work is on speech recognition and other forms of matching rather than generation of text.

We are not aware of these types of *n*-gram language models having been used for text corpus generation and we do not pursue them here.

1.6.3   NATURAL LANGUAGE GENERATION

A focus of natural language generation (NLG) methods is the generation of linguistically sensible text. Recurrent neural nets (RNNs) have been used for NLG. Their Long Short Term Memory (LSTM) variant models language structure more accurately, by modeling longer range dependencies. Sutskever et al. [83] and Karpathy [69] have demonstrated how this technique can, with appropriate training data, generate fragments of text which convincingly match the style of e.g., Shakespeare or a technical report. The resulting text conveys no real meaning but presents groups of words in plausible order, and with plausible punctuation.

Vaswani et al. [86] propose a new architecture, the Transformer, which focuses entirely on attention mechanisms and avoids the use of recurrence and convolutions. It is the model used in GPT-2 [67].

GPT-2 is "a large transformer-based language model with 1.5 billion parameters," released by OpenAI[7]: GPT-2 uses byte pair encodings (BPEs) on UTF-8 byte sequences.[8] With a byte sequence representation only a vocabulary of 256 entries is needed. There is no need to worry about pre-processing or tokenization. BPE merges frequently co-occurring byte pairs in a greedy fashion but GPT-2 prevents BPE from merging characters across categories (such as letters and punctuation, thus "dog" would not be merged with trailing punctuation). "GPT-2 is able to assign a probability to any Unicode string, regardless of any pre-processing steps."[9]

---

[6]Note that in this book we use *n*-gram to mean a sequence of *n* words, rather than a sequence of *n* letters.
[7]https://openai.com/blog/gpt-2-1-5b-release/
[8]https://www.topbots.com/generalized-language-models-bert-openai-gpt2/#bpe-on-byte-sequences
[9]Quoted from article referenced in Footnote 8.

A practical example of text generation by deep learning models is Google's Smart Compose, described by Chen et al. [20]. It is a service offered within Gmail to assist users to compose emails. The authors experimented with both LSTMs and with Transformer models.

As far as we are aware deep learning methods have not previously been applied to the generation of information retrieval test collections. In later chapters we report corpus emulation results obtained by fine-tuning GPT-2 on the TREC-AP corpus.

Deep learning techniques provide an exciting area of current research which holds great promise for greater fidelity of emulation, but for simulation of information retrieval test collections, there are a number of important questions to answer:

1. Much time and large computational resources (typically multiple GPUs) are required to train a model. Is this feasible for emulating a corpus such as ClueWeb12?

2. Once the model is built, is it possible to generate text at an adequate rate?

3. Will any increase in emulation fidelity come at the expense of greater leakage of confidential information?

4. Can the method also be used to emulate query logs?

We attempt to answer some of these questions in later chapters.

1.6.4   NATURAL LANGUAGE GENERATION FROM SEMANTICS

Quoting from Reiter and Dale [72], natural language generation:

> is concerned with the construction of computer systems that can produce understandable texts in English or other human languages from some underlying non-linguistic representation of information.

Sometimes probabilistic context free grammars are used to generate natural language text. Konstas and Lapata [55] describe such a system and we believe that SciGen[10] uses this method, with a hand-crafted grammar. SciGen is a system for generating fake academic papers. The authors take delight from the fact that some of the generated papers have been accepted at academic conferences.

The generation of artificial text which conveys real meaning seems at this point in time to be restricted to narrow semantic domains such as those listed in [73]: generating textual weather forecasts from weather maps, summarizing statistical data from a spreadsheet or database, and explaining medical information in a patient-friendly way. Another example is generating sports reports from the data about a game [19].

Natural language generation from semantics is beyond the scope of our work. In any case, any method for creating an emulated corpus by generating natural language text from the semantics of documents held by an organization would leak confidential information.

---

[10]https://pdos.csail.mit.edu/archive/scigen/

1.7   PRELIMINARY OBSERVATIONS ON METHODS

Most applications in the "experimenting with confidential data" area require sophisticated models, but are constrained by the need to maintain security of confidential information. A very accurate model might enable the deduction of important confidential information. For example, say $\mathbb{M}$ contained the fragment, "keep secret the security hole in ⟨name of flagship product⟩." Whether or not that sentence was accidentally quoted from the original corpus, it is likely that the original data set included information about keeping secrets and about security holes.

Even less blatant leakage may be problematic. For example, a sophisticated model may allow an attacker to determine that the sentence, "Our company will acquire company X" has higher probability than the sentence, "Our company will acquire company Y." It remains to be seen whether a useful balance can be struck between representational fidelity and preservation of privacy.

The more sophisticated models listed in Section 1.6 above remove the need to assume word independence but may require large models, resource intensive model training, and more CPU time and memory to generate words. Section 5.10 and Chapter 10 provide some empirical data on this.

For efficiency and scalability experimentation there are practical advantages in efficient generation, even if the modeling is less faithful to natural text. Smaller models allow easier sharing of experimental data with colleagues, and efficient generation of text enables faster experimental turn-around.

1.7.1   SIMULATION AS AN AID TO EFFICIENCY AND SCALABILITY EXPERIMENTATION

Studies of the efficiency of text indexing algorithms have often reported time and space results for the indexing of a single corpus such as GOV2 [24]. Examples include [54], [31], and many papers referenced in [94]. Empirically assessing the scalability of algorithms is difficult because of heterogeneity between corpora of different sizes. The size in bytes of one corpus may be x times larger than that of another but the ratio of the magnitude of the indexing tasks may be very different from x due to different vocabulary sizes, different word frequency distributions, and different proportions of indexable text.

Another limitation of past indexing efficiency studies is that published results are difficult to reproduce because of differences in details of how each indexer scans text. Indexers differ widely in the following aspects: recognition and conversion of character sets; stopword handling; word-break characters; stemming; parsing of markup; recognition and handling of text in "fields;" handling of comments and no-index sections, obedience to "robots" metatags; indexing of element attributes; recognition of XML entities; and handling of mark-up which isn't well-formed. Simulation can be used to produce corpora which avoid these issues.

There is now community interest in the study of memory-resident indexing and retrieval algorithms for Non-Uniform Memory Access (NUMA) architectures. Since 2010 or so, it has been possible to purchase off-the-shelf servers configured with multiple terabytes of RAM. Such servers are characterized by great variations in memory access speed, due to multiple levels of cache, to the need to maintain cache coherency, and to the closer association of banks of RAM to just one of several CPU chips. For example, the best access latency in clock cycles for different levels of memory in the Intel Core i7 Xeon 5500 series is 4 for L1 cache, 10 for L2 cache, 40 for L3 cache, 60 for local DRAM, and 100 for remote DRAM.[11]

Meaningful empirical comparison of retrieval algorithms in NUMA environments requires large corpora, which are difficult to share with others—test collections like ClueWeb 09 have been shared in the past by the cumbersome means of shipping arrays of hard disks.

Logically, a synthetic corpus derived from a real one may be considered to be a lossily compressed version of the original. Instead of shipping hard disks of text data we can ship a potentially much smaller model plus a small set of parameters, a random seed, and give access to the generator code (e.g., corpusGenerator).

The compression factor can be increased significantly if we generate the word representations, and mathematically model the word probability distribution rather than recording a full histogram. In the Baseline algorithm presented in Section 1.5.2, if the random number generator picks say word 13507, then we look up the word table in the language model and find that that corresponds to adumbrate. If we instead generate the word representations, then an algorithm maps word number 13507 to a unique sequence of characters rather than to a known word. For example, it may generate xxrp2. Note that a word representation generator may be needed to solve a limitation mentioned above—that scaling up a corpus should not assume a fixed vocabulary. The corpusGenerator tool provides a range of different methods for producing word representations.

Synthetic corpora can be used for studies of efficiency and scalability of indexing algorithms. Combined with simulated known-item queries or emulated query logs, synthetic corpora can potentially also be used to study the efficiency of query processing algorithms. Indeed, since known item queries provide for limited evaluation without the need for human judgments, it is possible to simulate test collections and to use them to compare and tune retrieval methods.

1.8   RESOURCES USED IN EXPERIMENTS

This monograph presents the results of a great deal of empirical work. Here we document important datasets, hardware, and software used in these experiments.

1.8.1   DATASETS

We base most of our empirical work on the TREC base corpora documented in Table 1.1. All but one are very familiar to participants in TREC Ad Hoc and TREC Web Tracks from the 1990s. Readers who are unfamiliar are referred to "the TREC book" [87].

---

[11]https://software.intel.com/en-us/forums/intel-manycore-testing-lab/topic/287236 accessed January 7, 2016.

Table 1.1: Details of the principal TREC corpora used throughout this work. Note that the corpora were passed through the DETREC program to convert text into sequences of "indexable words" encoded in UTF-8, without formatting or punctuation. Please see page xxi for an explanation of symbols.

Corpus	N	P	$|V|$
TREC-AP	242,892	113 M	308,037
TREC-WSJ	173,252	81 M	234,015
TREC-FR	55,632	39 M	265,431
TREC-PAT	6,711	35 M	280,953
TREC-all	1,634,044	775 M	1,832,917
WT10g	1,687,888	1,037 M	5,398,213
T8 NLQs	199,794	1.2 M	47,929

It is relatively easy for researchers who don't already have them to obtain the TREC corpora via trec.nist.gov. WT10g is currently distributed by the University of Glasgow (http://ir.dcs.gla.ac.uk/test_collections/wt10g.html).

The T8 NLQs corpus comprises approximately 200,000 natural language web queries used in the TREC-8 Web Track in 1999. They were included because of our interest in indexing and querying corpora of very short texts. They were provided by the now-defunct Alta Vista and Electric Monk web search engines and contain no session, timestamp, or userid information. They were submitted to a question answering interface. Here is a sample:

```
what is the origin of the statue of liberty ?
Where I can I buy pictures of U.S. Presidents?
who are cdic
Where can I rent an RV in Binghamton, NY?
microforum
what effect does dietary sodium have on blood pressure?
British & American Racing
```

To broaden the generality of our work, we also report some observations on the properties of the corpora detailed in Table 1.2. These include two different subsets of the ClueWeb12 corpus and a number of corpora which were available inside Microsoft.

When making timing and resource comparisons of an IR system on base and emulated versions of the same corpus, we need to remove the confounding effect of mark-up and character encodings present in the base but not in the emulated version. Accordingly, we developed a program DETREC[12] to convert TREC corpora to UTF-8 and strip markup, leaving only indexable

---

[12]DETREC is included in the SYNTHACORPUS project at https://bitbucket.org/davidhawking/synthacorpus/.

Table 1.2: Details of other larger or internal-to-Microsoft corpora for which some observations are presented in this work

Corpus	N	$|V|$	P	Description
Popular queries	100.00 M	6.41 M	381.0 M	Popular Web queries
Song lyrics	27.92 M	0.91 M	153.0 M	Song lyric lines
Wikipedia titles	11.06 M	2.32 M	32.7 M	Wikipedia titles (inc. redirects)
Academic paper titles	89.53 M	11.98 M	1003.6 M	Collection of paper titles
ClueWeb12 titles	728.88 M	21.78 M	5687.3 M	ClueWeb12 document titles
ClueWeb12 bodies	23.30 M	61.11 M	5340.1 M	Subset of ClueWeb12 bodies
Tweets	710.62 M	340.75 M	8843.7 M	Daily Twitter samples

```
<DOC>
<DOCNO> AP880212-0001 </DOCNO>
<TEXT>
Reports Former Saigon Officials Released from Re education
Camp More than 150 former officers of the overthrown South
Vietnamese government have been released from a re education
camp after 13 years of detention the official Vietnam News
Agency reported Saturday
...
</TEXT>
</DOC>
```

Figure 1.4: A fragment of a TREC-AP document after processing by DETREC.

words and minimal mark-up (DOC, DOCNO, and TEXT elements). In the case of web pages this means that hyperlinks, scripts, styles, and all markup are removed. An indexable word is essentially a maximal sequence of letters and digits, but is truncated to a maximum length. In our experiments the maximum was set at 15 Unicode characters. Very long words which share the same initial 15 characters are treated as the same word.

Base and emulated corpora are in identical format. The data for corpora TREC-AP, TREC-FR, TREC-PAT, T8 NLQs, and WT10g listed in Table 1.1 relate to versions processed by DETREC.

Figure 1.4 illustrates the format produced by DETREC.

1.8.2   HARDWARE

Almost all of the experimental runs in this book were performed using one or other of the MacBook Pro configurations detailed in Figure 1.5. Both of them are fitted with sufficient solid state

macOS Catalina
Version 10.15.3

MacBook Pro (16-inch, 2019)
Processor   2.4 GHz 8-Core Intel Core i9
Memory   64 GB 2667 MHz DDR4

(a) NewMac

macOS Catalina
Version 10.15.3

MacBook Pro (Retina, 15-inch, Early 2013)
Processor   2.8 GHz Quad-Core Intel Core i7
Memory   16 GB 1600 MHz DDR3

(b) OldMac

Figure 1.5: Specifications of two MacBook Pro systems used in experiments reported here.

disk (SSD) storage to accommodate all the experimentation on the principal corpora. NewMac is somewhat faster than OldMac. Its much larger memory configuration would be an advantage for large-scale experiments, but for the corpora in Table 1.1, is only needed when building high-order Markov models.

A small number of experiments on larger corpora were performed on large-scale servers running Windows. We will reference them as "FujitsuServer" and "HPServer," respectively.

Fujitsu Primergy RX900 S2 CPUs: 8 x Intel Xeon E7-8850 @ 2.0 GHz (2.4 GHz turbo), each with 10 cores per CPU, Westmere 32 nm technology, 24 MB Smart-Cache. RAM: 4TB total, 512 GB per NUMA node. DDR3 @ 1600 MHz

HP Proliant DL380 Gen 9 CPUs: 2 x Intel Xeon E5-2643 v3 @ 3.4 GHz (3.7 GHz turbo), each with 6 cores per CPU, Haswell 22 nm technology, 20 MB L3 Cache. RAM: 512 GB total, 256 GB per NUMA node. DDR3 @ 1600 MHz GPU: Nvidia Tesla K80 (2 x Kepler GK210, each with 2496 CUDA cores, and 12 GB of GDDR5 RAM)

1.8.3   CORPUS GENERATOR SOFTWARE

Table 1.3 lists the five generators provided by SYNTHACORPUS. We also generate a GPT-2 corpus based on the 774 million parameter model from OpenAI. Before generating unconditional samples the model is fine tuned with the TREC-AP collection. To ensure GPT-2 is comparable with the TREC-AP collection we generate the same number of documents (242,892) with the average document length (465 words per document), as shown in Table 1.1. Other than there not being any variability in document lengths in this simulated collection, documents generated this way generally also differ in that the generation process stops mid-sentence when the requested number of words is reached.

Finally, in our experiments in Chapter 9 we use a simple copy (/bin/cp) utility to quantify how much uncontrolled variation in timing results is inherent due to disk layout etc.

Table 1.3: The corpus generators implemented in SynthaCorpus

Generator	Description
Caesar	Encryption by letter substitution
Nomenclator	Encryption by word substitution
WBMarkov	Order 0 and order 1 generation based on word probabilities
stringMarkovGen	Up to order 48 generation based on letter probabilities
CorpusGenerator	Generates a corpus with specified macro-level properties. Supports a range of choices for each modeling dimension

1.9   OUTLINE OF THE MONOGRAPH

Chapter 2 presents methods for assessing the fidelity of a corpus emulation, including visual inspection, and Jensen–Shannon divergence. These methods are employed in assessing the modeling used in following chapters.

In Chapter 3, we consider a range of models for document length distribution. In Chapter 4, we explore models of word probability distribution, assuming independence. In Chapter 5, we look at term dependence models, and the important question of how to measure whether the associations between terms have been properly modeled. Chapter 6 discusses the generation of sequences of characters to represent words, when it is not possible to use the lexicon of a corpus being emulated.

In Chapter 7, we show how the characteristics of samples of each corpus change as we increase the size of the samples from 1% up to 100%. From these observations we derive growth models and report scaling-up experiments which attempt to emulate $\mathbb{B}$ from the average properties of a number of samples of $\mathbb{B}$. Fidelity is less than in the direct emulation case, but the results are still quite promising.

Chapter 8 discusses published methods for generating corpus-compatible queries and judgments, and also for simulating query logs. Implementations of these methods are distributed with SynthaCorpus. Chapter 9 studies how well efficiency and effectiveness measurements taken on emulated corpora predict those taken on a real corpus, for three different open-source retrieval engines. Chapter 10 measures the speed of generation of text corpora and of known-item query sets, for the different simulation methods. Chapter 11 discusses emulation methods in the context of leakage of confidential information, while Chapter 12 presents overall discussion and conclusions.

In the Information Retrieval field it is common to use the term "term" to refer to words. Here we also use it to refer to compounds such as n-grams. When we are specifically talking about words, we use the word "word" rather than the term "term."

CHAPTER 2

Evaluation Approaches

Chapters 3–6 present alternative approaches to each of the major corpus modeling dimensions. These approaches vary in their ability to faithfully model a corpus; some of the approaches can be more or less faithful depending upon settings such as the number of segments in a piecewise linear model. There is a clear need to devise suitable evaluation methodologies for comparing different approaches and for measuring how faithfully an emulated collection matches the corresponding real one.

2.1 TASK-BASED EVALUATION

In practical use, the most relevant forms of evaluation are those derived from the task for which the emulated collection was created.

- How well are observations on a real collection (e.g., indexing speed, query response latency, ranking accuracy etc.) predicted by observations on a simulated collection?

When working with a private corpus, the ability to accurately predict real behavior on the dimensions we care about is all we care about. We need to be able to do this in the presence of constraints on what we are allowed to extract from the private data.

Chapter 9 presents some illustrative evaluations along these lines, using open-source IR systems and TREC datasets. Measurements on several dimensions are taken on various emulations of the original datasets and compared with the measurements from the originals. In that chapter we make use of the *prediction accuracy ratio* R_1 which is the ratio of the smaller observation to the larger. This gives us a number between 0 and 1. Using this form of ratio we can meaningfully average observations across multiple measurement dimensions, such as indexing speed, query processing rate, and retrieval accuracy, to give an overall score for the fidelity of emulation.

When trying to estimate required computing hardware resources another ratio R_2, the ratio of a measurement obtained by simulation to the real measurement, is needed, because it is important to know whether the simulated measurement is an over-estimate or an under-estimate of the real one.

Another thing to keep in mind when measuring the prediction accuracy of a simulation method based on a random number generator, is that the accuracy may vary depending upon the sequence of random numbers. In Chapter 9, we average accuracies obtained across a number of random trials and also explore the distribution of accuracy scores across a large number of trials.

2.2   NON-TASK-BASED EVALUATION

Task-based evaluation allows us to measure the end-to-end performance of a simulation but we may need finer-grained evaluations to understand why observations from a simulated collection fail to accurately predict behavior on a real system. For example, if we observe that indexing of a base corpus $\mathbb{B}$ is substantially faster or slower than indexing of an emulated version $\mathbb{M}$, we may want to look at individual modeling dimensions, such as vocabulary sizes, word-frequency distributions, document-length distributions, and word-length distributions, etc. of $\mathbb{M}$ and $\mathbb{B}$. If we find that one dimension is much less accurately modeled than others, we may be able to improve the prediction accuracy by replacing that model with a better one.

Some of the modeling parameters are simple numeric quantities and can be easily compared. However, others are distributions and we need more sophisticated methods to compare them.

2.2.1   COMPARING DISTRIBUTIONS: VISUAL METHOD

A method which will be used extensively in subsequent chapters is that of plotting two distributions on a single set of axes, often log-log, in order to allow visual comparison.

Visual comparison has the advantage that it may give a very clear indication (see Figure 3.1 for example) of how two distributions differ—whether the plots have different shapes, whether the slopes of the lines differ, or whether the domains of the plots are radically different.

In many cases the independent variable in a plot takes discrete rather than continuous values. Although not mathematically justified, we sometimes connect the points of the graph with lines in order to make relationships clearer.

As previously noted, a corpus generated by random sampling is only one of an infinite number of possible outcomes. Distributional plots for different corpora generated with the same generation parameters are likely to vary.

It should not be forgotten that visual comparisons depend upon how the data is plotted: whether the data is plotted on logarithmic or linear axes; what range of values is chosen for the horizontal axis; and how a suitable subset of millions of data points is chosen for plotting. These choices can radically change the form of the plots, potentially obscuring important differences, or magnifying less important ones.

Similar considerations apply when calculating lines of best fit. If all of the points in a Zipfian distribution are taken into account, the line of best fit will be biased toward the tail, while a sample may bias it toward the head.

As long as caution is used and the distributions are plotted appropriately visual comparison can be a very useful method, arguably the most useful.

On the other hand, visual comparison has the disadvantage that it doesn't result in a single-dimensional measure of difference. This is a limitation when we want to choose between different emulation methods—Which of them is more accurate? To support this usage, we make use of a single-number measure to assess the difference between discrete probability distributions.

2.2.2   COMPARING DISTRIBUTIONS: SINGLE-NUMBER MEASURES

It is very useful to have a single-number measure of the degree of difference between two discrete probability distributions, e.g., occurrence probabilities for words. Such a measure enables us to say that fidelity of emulation of the word frequency distribution is higher in one emulation than another, in circumstances where it is difficult to determine by visual inspection.

Something to keep in mind is that, if $\mathbb{M}$ results from a random process, the measured degree of difference between its word frequency distribution and that of $\mathbb{B}$ applies only to that specific generated instance. To correctly measure the fidelity of an emulation method, one would have to generate a large number of $\mathbb{M}$s and average the difference measures.

Usually, in language modeling work, M_i and B_i relate to the same word. That is not generally the case in corpus synthesis, where the vocabularies of $\mathbb{M}$ and $\mathbb{B}$ may be completely different. In our work we rank the words in order of descending frequency and compare the probabilities of whatever words appear at the same rank.

When we want to measure differences between probability distributions for word frequencies, n-gram frequencies, co-occurrence frequencies, self-co-occurrence frequencies, document lengths, and word lengths, we use the same ranking approach. Note that we are interested in reporting and comparing differences between distributions rather than testing significance.

We considered four alternative difference measures. **Kullback–Leibler divergence (KLD)**[1]: KLD can give us an information theoretic measure of the extent to which a discrete probability distribution M diverges from another B:

$$\mathrm{KLD}(M||B) = \sum_{\forall i} M_i \log_2 \frac{M_i}{B_i}.$$

The contribution of the i-th elements to KLD is zero if either $M_i = 0$ or $B_i = 0$. Missing elements are considered to be zero.

A problem with KLD is that it is assymetrical ($\mathrm{KLD}(M||B) \neq \mathrm{KLD}(B||M)$) and has no clearly defined upper bound. Furthermore, whenever $M_i < B_i$ the contribution of that pair of elements to KLD is negative because the log of a proper fraction is negative. That seems counter-intuitive.

Jensen–Shannon divergence (JSD)[2]: JSD is based on KLD but is symmetric and lies in the range 0–1. It also addresses the issue of the negative contributions:

$$\mathrm{JSD}(M||B) = \frac{\mathrm{KLD}(M||J) + \mathrm{KLD}(B||J)}{2},$$

where

$$J = \frac{M + B}{2}.$$

[1] https://en.wikipedia.org/wiki/Kullback-Leibler_divergence
[2] https://en.wikipedia.org/wiki/Jensen-Shannon_divergence

Bhattacharyya distance (BD)[3]: BD is another symmetric measure of the distance between two distributions. Its range is 0–∞.

$$BD(M, B) = -\log BC(M, B),$$

where

$$BC(M, B) = \sum_{\forall i} \sqrt{M_i B_i}.$$

Kolmogorov–Smirnov statistic (KSS)[4]: Informally, KSS measures the greatest vertical gap between the two cumulative probability distributions. It is symmetric and its range is 0–1. One undesirable aspect of KSS when comparing arrays of values is that it depends upon the order of the elements of the arrays. In general, KSS values may change if both M and B are permuted in the same way. That's not true for any of the other three measures.

Choice of Measure

Eliminating KLD because of its asymetry and the issue of negative contributions, and KSS because of its dependence upon data permutation, left us with a choice between JSD and BD. We decided to use JSD because it's more widely used in the Information Retrieval literature and because we preferred its 0–1 range.

Unfortunately JSD, like KLD and BD, has a serious weakness when the two distributions have very different numbers of points. One might expect that the fact that one distribution has four times as many points as the other would result in a large JSD score, but in fact the surplus data points play no role in the difference calculation. This is because any term missing or zero from Y in $KLD(X||Y)$ must be excluded from the KLD calculation, and because JSD uses both $KLD(X||Y)$ and $KLD(Y||X)$.

In the following chapters you will see quite a few examples where two distributions seem very different visually, but where the JSD score is quite small.

---

[3] https://en.wikipedia.org/wiki/Bhattacharyya_distance
[4] https://en.wikipedia.org/wiki/Kolmogorov-Smirnov_test

CHAPTER 3

Modeling Document Lengths

In some applications, very approximate modeling of the distribution of document lengths will suffice. However, there are many scenarios in which accurate modeling is desirable. For example, significant gains in retrieval effectiveness were achieved at TREC-3 through better normalization of document length [74, 81]. Those effects could not have been observed on a simulated collection in which all documents had the same length. Furthermore, distributions of term co-occurrences, distributions of TFs, and topic mixtures are all affected by the distribution of document lengths.

Finally, the efficiency of some indexing or query processing algorithms may be affected by very long or very short documents. For example, the choice between inverted file and signature methods may depend upon the distribution of document lengths.

We have studied several different document length models. In the following, the length of a document is defined as the number of indexable words it contains. First let us consider the distribution of lengths arising from Markov processes.

3.1   LENGTHS ARISING FROM MARKOV PROCESSES

In our Markov document generators, EOD is treated as an extra symbol, and its probability of occurrence is calculated and used in the same way as for other symbols. In WBMARKOV1 the corpus is considered to be preceded by an implicit EOD. In the case of STRINGMARKOVGEN with order k, each document is considered to be preceded by k EODs.

To study the document-length distributions arising from Markov processes, we used the TREC-AP corpus as an example and emulated it by running the Markov generators until they produced exactly the same number of word occurrences in $\mathbb{M}$ as in $\mathbb{B}$. If necessary, end of document markup was emitted to finalise the last document in $\mathbb{M}$.

Because the generation process is random, the number of documents in $\mathbb{M}$ will vary depending upon choice of the random seed. We performed ten emulations for both WBMARKOV0 and WBMARKOV1. Table 3.1 reports the mean and range of the numbers observed as percentages of the number of documents in $\mathbb{B}$. The numbers of documents generated show quite small variability and are close to the numbers in $\mathbb{B}$. However, Figure 3.1 shows that the distributions of document lengths for $\mathbb{M}$ and $\mathbb{B}$ differ greatly. Inspection of the two plots for the emulated corpora fails to reveal any obvious difference between the order zero and order one models.

Table 3.1: Variation in number of documents generated in WBMarkov emulations of the TREC-AP corpus. Ten trials were conducted for each method and the number of documents generated in each case was expressed as a percentage of the number in the base corpus $\mathbb{B}$. This table shows the mean, standard deviation, and range of those percentages.

(a) WBMARKOV0		(b) WBMARKOV1	
Mean/St.Dev	Range	Mean/St.Dev	Range
99.98/0.22	99.53–100.19	99.69/0.16	99.40–99.97

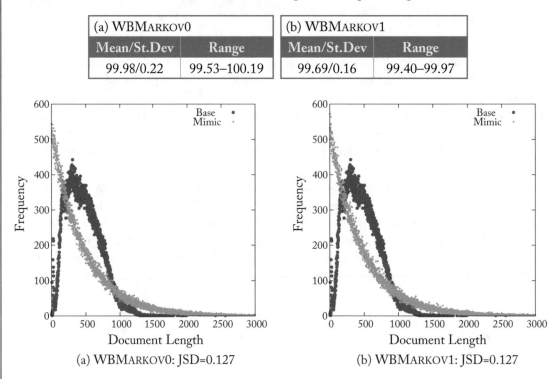

(a) WBMARKOV0: JSD=0.127   (b) WBMARKOV1: JSD=0.127

Figure 3.1: Distribution of document lengths in $\mathbb{M}$ (Mimic) and $\mathbb{B}$ (Base) resulting from single WBMARKOV emulations of the TREC-AP corpus.

Emulation of TREC-AP using STRINGMARKOVGEN with $k = 23$ shows very similar document length distributions to the WBMARKOV models. Again the number of documents in $\mathbb{M}$ is very close to that in $\mathbb{B}$.

Since the "bottom-up" Markov generators do a very poor job of modeling the distribution of document lengths, let's take a top-down look and try to fit models to the distribution.

3.2 FITTING LENGTH MODELS

3.2.1 LEFT-TRUNCATED GAUSSIAN MODEL

The mean and standard deviation of document lengths in the primary corpus are easily calculated. We can then sample lengths from a normal distribution with those parameters using an appropriate function such as ceil() to convert real values to integer lengths. If a zero or negative length is sampled it is rejected, leading to a shift in the actual mean of the truncated distribution. CORPUSGENERATOR applies heuristic multiplicative correction factors to both mean and standard deviation to more accurately model the primary corpus.

CORPUSGENERATOR makes use of the efficient method for generation of normally distributed random numbers due to Marsaglia and Bray [59].

We found that for many corpora the truncated normal distribution significantly undergenerates longer documents found in the original distribution. Furthermore, we see no theoretical reason to expect that document lengths ought to be normally distributed. Therefore, apart from implementation convenience, there is little to recommend this model.

3.2.2   GAMMA DISTRIBUTION MODEL

A gamma distribution can be specified using two real parameters—shape and scale. Depending upon the values of these parameters the form of the distribution can approximate normal, exponential, uniform, and other forms. This flexibility allows gamma to model observed length distributions for many real corpora with greater fidelity than was the case with the Gaussian. Unlike the Gaussian, gamma can emulate the heavy tail found in many observed document length distributions. We note that Zobel et al. [95] used the gamma distribution for modeling document lengths.

We estimated the parameters for a gamma distribution using the method and code due to Minka et al. [64, 65].[1] We implemented sampling from a specified Gamma distribution using the efficient method of Marsaglia and Tsang [60]. The gamma distribution can achieve good fidelity on some corpora, requires only two parameters, and can easily control the generation of a corpus much larger than the original.

3.2.3   GEOMETRIC AND NEGATIVE BINOMIAL MODELS

If we added an EOD symbol to our word distribution and emitted it with fixed probability $1 - p$, then each act of sampling would constitute a Bernoulli trial in which the emission of an end-of-document symbol represents the "failure."[2] In this scheme, the number of successes (i.e., length of document in words) before a failure would be geometrically distributed.

However, a geometric distribution has only one parameter, the probability of success. In this model, the probability of a document having a particular length monotonically decreases with the length—the length with the highest probability is zero. This pattern can be clearly seen in Figure 3.1.

These observations seem to refute the hypothesis that the length of a document is determined by the author conducting Bernoulli trials.

---

[1]Downloadable from http://infernet.azurewebsites.net/ (Microsoft.Infer.Distributions).
[2]This is exactly what happens in our Markov generators.

A negative binomial distribution represents the probability of each possible number of successes before r failures, i.e., the author experiences a number of possible stopping points and only ends the document at the r-th such point. For larger values of r this distribution does not monotically decrease and zero words is no longer the most probable length. In effect the negative binomial variable can be considered as the concatenation of r consecutive experiments associated with a geometric distribution.

3.2.4   COMPARISON OF MODELS

We used the FITDISTRPLUS R package [30] to fit models to the observed data for various corpora. Figure 3.2 show the results. There is no clear winner, but negative binomial and gamma are generally better than truncated normal. However, none of the models is capable of modeling a multimodal distribution. Several of the plots in Figure 3.2 provide examples of such a distribution. For example, the plots for TREC-AP and TREC-FR show that each has a bimodal distribution with a pronounced spike at quite short lengths.

Multimodal distributions of document lengths seem to be reasonably common and may correspond to corpora consisting of a mixture of document types, e.g., a mixture of abstracts and articles.

When all the TREC Ad Hoc corpora are combined (TREC-all comprising all five TREC Ad Hoc CD-ROMs, including TREC-AP, TREC-FR, and TREC-PAT), the document length distribution appears quite regular.

However, different corpora have very different length distributions. Documents in T8 NLQs are naturally short and their distribution of lengths is quite well modeled by any of the three distributions. The distribution of lengths for TREC-PAT in Figure 3.2 is highly scattered, though bucketing or using a much larger sample of patent documents would reduce the scattering. TREC-PAT includes some very long documents.

One approach would be to model the observed distribution as a mixture of two or more distributions and fit the data using a maximum likelihood method.[3] We have not yet attempted that. Instead, we explored piecewise linear models as a means of fitting multi-modal or irregularly distributed data.

3.2.5   PIECEWISE LINEAR LENGTH MODEL

Initial experiments with piecewise segments defined as either fixed intervals on the horizontal axis or fixed areas under the curve were unsatisfactory. Fine segments were needed to model perturbations in the curve, resulting in large models.

We next tried an adaptive method. We bucketed document lengths and started with a single segment extending from the first bucket to the last. We then recursively split it at the

---

[3]Baeza-Yates and Navarro [6] report that the distribution of web page sizes, including non-text files can be modeled by a combination of log normal and Pareto distributions.

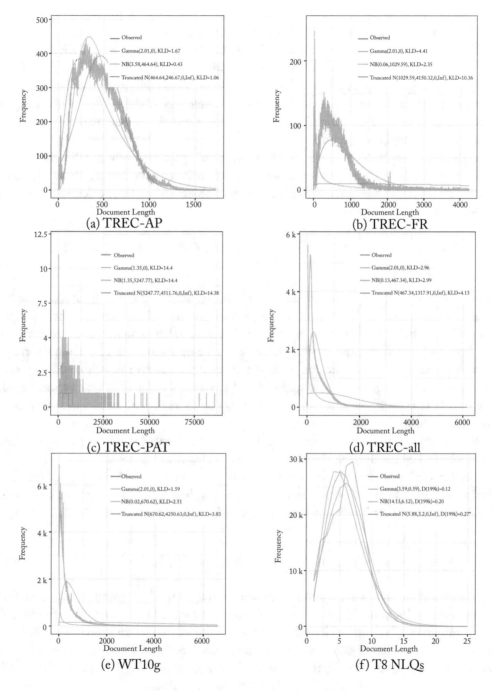

Figure 3.2: Different document length models applied to several corpora.

bucket where the deviation of actual frequency from the predicted by the line segment was at a maximum, provided that deviation was larger than a threshold.

Results of this process are shown in Figure 3.3. In some cases, e.g., TREC-all and T8 NLQs the modeling is quite accurate, however for other corpora such as WT10g and TREC-PAT the modeling is less successful. We were unable to find a combination of bucket size and split threshold which achieved sufficient modeling accuracy on all the corpora while using only a modest number of segments. Small bucket sizes were needed to model narrow peaks but led to jitter and large numbers of segments.

Given that the piecewise linear model provides no explanatory power, relies on heuristics, and requires a relatively large number of parameters to achieve good results across corpora, we proceeded to investigate using the actual histogram of observed lengths, bucketed and/or scaled up as necessary.

3.3   LENGTH MODELS RELYING ON OBSERVED HISTOGRAMS

In some applications, it may be acceptable to use a histogram of observed document lengths for an original corpus, even with a bucket size of 1. If the number of distinct document lengths is high then it may be preferable to use a larger bucket size. When generating document lengths from a bucketed histogram, the lengths chosen could be uniformly sampled from the range of lengths represented by the bucket or perhaps a fixed representative length could be emitted. There would be advantage to using a dynamic bucket-sizing scheme which uses narrow buckets for the shorter lengths where accurate modeling may be more important and increases them in arithmetic, geometric or other sequence.

Scaling up a histogram in order to generate a corpus larger (or smaller) than the original is easily achieved by multiplying the bucket counts by a constant factor.

Perfect fidelity can be achieved when emulation uses an unscaled, unbucketed length histogram from the original corpus. A limitation when scaling up is that, without some sort of smoothing, there is no possibility of generating lengths which were not observed in the original corpus.

3.4   IMPLEMENTATION IN SYNTHACORPUS

corpusGenerator supports a number of document length models: uniform, truncated Gaussian, Gamma distribution, piecewise linear segments, and scaled histogram. In each case it first builds a histogram of document lengths and then, from it, derives an array giving the length of every document in the corpus. Initially, the array may contain 50 instances of length 1, 100 instances of length 2, etc. but then it is shuffled to mix up the lengths. An in-place random shuffling algorithm due to Durstenfield [32][4] runs in linear time.

[4]It is a more efficient version of the Fisher–Yates method and is also known as Knuth shuffle.

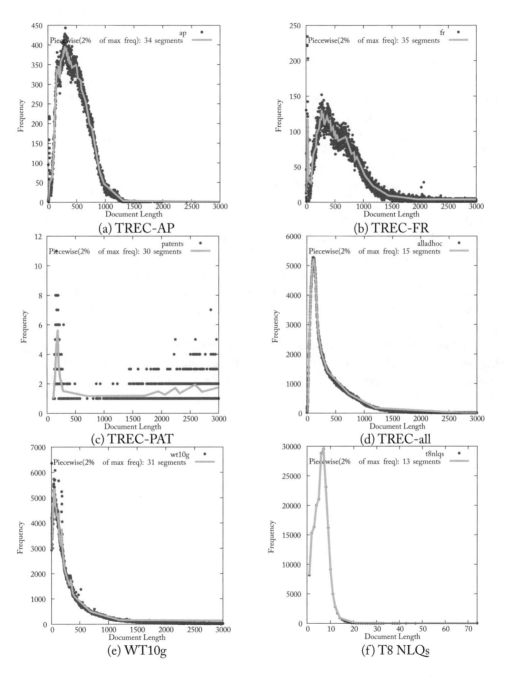

Figure 3.3: Results of piecewise linear modeling of document lengths in our principal corpora.

In the unscaled histogram case, we are effectively sampling without replacement—the histogram of document lengths in $\mathbb{M}$ will be identical to that for $\mathbb{B}$. However, in the piecewise linear, truncated Gaussian, and Gamma cases, the generator keeps sampling lengths from the relevant distribution until the total of the lengths is at least as great as the requested total number of word occurrences. This is sampling with replacement—some document lengths found in $\mathbb{B}$ may not be found in $\mathbb{M}$. We don't see that as a major short-coming, but a possible future code improvement would be to sample without replacement by mapping areas under the model curve to numbers of documents of a given length, following the approach taken for word frequency modeling in Sections 4.3 and 4.4.

3.5   LENGTH MODELS: WHICH TO CHOOSE?

In this chapter we have presented the document-length distributions for several corpora and shown how well they can be modeled by the different approaches we have considered.

We recommend choosing the gamma model if mathematical simplicity and a small number of parameters is desired, unless the observed length distribution for the primary corpus is clearly multi-modal. It would be possible to model a distribution as a mixture of gamma distributions, perhaps by splitting the corpus into sub-corpora, e.g., abstracts and articles, and modeling them separately.

In other circumstances, the use of a histogram-based method is preferred despite being a highly-overfitted model. The optimal bucketing scheme and whether to implement some form of smoothing should be determined after analysis of the data and the intended application.

CHAPTER 4

Modeling Word Frequencies, Assuming Independence

The distribution of word frequencies has a big effect on the design of efficient text retrieval systems. Schemes for reducing the size of indexes, for matching phrases, and for efficiently processing queries of all types are designed around the observation that in most real text corpora thousands of words occur only once while a few words may account for more than half of all word occurrences. If the word frequency distribution of $\mathbb{M}$ differs substantially from that of $\mathbb{B}$ the behavior of a retrieval system may differ substantially between them.

We start our discussion of word frequency distributions by exploring the use of the full language model and the BASELINE algorithm and then move on to a model which is considerably more sophisticated, though it still assumes word independence.

4.1 GENERATING TEXT WITH THE BASELINE ALGORITHM

As noted in the introduction we can use a cumulative word probability histogram as the basis for word-id generation. We have done this for the Academic paper titles corpus described in Table 4.1. We used the BASELINE algorithm to generate simulated corpora of 10%, 100%, and 1000% of the number of postings in the original corpus. The cumulative word probability histogram was derived from the full Academic paper titles corpus.

To test that our algorithm and the underlying pseudo-random number generator (Mersenne Twister [61], Tiny 64bit version) were working correctly we predicted what percentage of singleton words in the language model would fail to be selected in $P = 1004$ million draws—the number of postings in the Academic paper titles corpus. Since each draw has a $(P-1)/P$ probability of missing a particular singleton and there are P draws, we can raise $(P-1)/P$ to the power of P to get the probability of missing a singleton entirely. The predicted and observed proportions of missed singletons were 0.36785 and 0.36788, respectively, showing agreement to 4 decimal places. Part of the small disagreement may be due to BASELINE missing not only singletons but also words with higher frequency through the same process. The net effect is a significant overall loss of vocabulary for $\mathbb{M}_{100\%}$.

Table 4.1: Emulation of academic paper titles corpus using the BASELINE algorithm

Corpus	P	$|V|$	Singletons
$\mathbb{B}$	1004 M	11.98 M	7.187 M
$\mathbb{M}_{10\%}$	100.4 M	2.715 M	1.676 M
$\mathbb{M}_{100\%}$	1004 M	9.053 M	3.256 M
$\mathbb{M}_{1000\%}$	10040 M	11.98 M	0.003 M

The results for BASELINE are tabulated in Table 4.1. When simulating a corpus of the same size as $\mathbb{B}$ the vocabulary size is only 76% as large as the original. The under-generation of the vocabulary occurs essentially because we are sampling words from the model *with replacement*.[1]

When the number of samples drawn from the language model is increased by a factor of ten ($\mathbb{M}_{1000\%}$) virtually all the words are selected. This confirms that the random number generator has sufficient resolution. However, the vocabulary size cannot and does not exceed the size of the model and the number of singleton words reduces to almost zero (because former singletons are drawn more than once).

A better approach to emulation would involve sampling *without replacement*. Implemented using rejection, this might be impractically slow, but fast implementations are possible, most obviously using the same approach as recommended for the document length histograms. That is, expand the histogram into an array of word occurrences and shuffle it using Durstenfeld's algorithm. This approach is taken in CORPUSGENERATOR. In Table 4.1, the numbers in the $\mathbb{M}_{100\%}$ row would have been identical to those in the $\mathbb{B}$ row, had sampling without replacement been used.

The model sizes for the BASELINE algorithm are large. In the case of the Academic paper titles corpus, the size of the model is approximately 12 million elements, each comprising a text string and a high-precision probability value. For the Tweets corpus the corresponding figure would be more than 340 million elements.

4.2   MODELING WORD FREQUENCY DISTRIBUTIONS

Many believe that the word probability distribution in a text corpus follows Zipf's law [93]. That law states that the probability $\Pr(t_r)$ of the r-th most frequent word is proportional to a negative power α of the rank r. Miller [63] claims that "text" generated by monkeys on typewriters approximates Zipf's law provided only that the probability of hitting space is constant (approximately 0.18) and that spaces never appear consecutively.

---

[1]See footnote 5 on p. 9.

We can relate Zipf's law to a continuous probability function in which r is real:

$$\Pr(t_r) \propto r^{\alpha}.$$

If this model applied perfectly, a log-log plot of probability against rank would show a negatively sloping straight line. However, it is frequently observed that real-world frequency distributions conform to Zipf's law less well at both high and the low frequencies. For example, Baeza-Yates [5] reports that singleton queries are far more heavily represented in query frequency distributions than would be predicted by a power law which fits the upper part of the distribution.

A considerable literature has accumulated describing approaches to achieving better modeling of such "Zipfian" distributions. Baeza-Yates and Navarro [6] mention a slight advantage to the use of a Mandelbrot distribution. Laherrère [57], discussing sizes of oilfields, proposes a "parabolic fractal" model which would lead to a quadratic fit in log-log space. Figures 4.1 and 4.2 show log-log plots of word probability against rank along with both linear and quadratic lines of best fit.

Note that only a subset of points are shown—the full number of points is too large to display. Least squares fitting is carried out on the plotted subset of points. The points in the subset were chosen such that each point in the subset was at least a small distance ϵ (in log-log space) away from the others. The number of points was thus reduced to the order of one thousand rather than tens or hundreds of millions. One effect of this procedure is to reduce the bias of fitting toward the tail due to its huge preponderance of points.

More recently, Petersen et al. [68] have conducted a very comprehensive data fitting study of distributions in IR. For nearly all of 28 different IR corpora they found that, of 16 different models of the word frequency distribution, the Yule–Pareto was the best-fitting discrete model and Generalized Extreme Value (GEV) the best-fitting continuous one. In Figure 3 of their paper, Petersen et al. graph the results of fitting on four of the corpora. It's interesting to note that in the case of the iSearch and ClueWeb12 cat. B corpora their GEV line of best fit closely matches the head section of the plot but deviates markedly in the middle section.[2]

Even more recently, Chierichetti et al. [23] describe a word frequency distribution as two fused power laws with a curved transition between them, i.e., the head part of the curve is modeled by a power law and the tail by another whose slope is steeper. Chierichetti et al. present a two-stage generative process which they show leads to better modeling of a real corpus than a double Pareto model. However, three of the four corpora modeled in their Figure 5 show quite marked deviations between observation and model in the first few head points.

None of the models we are aware of give accurate fit for all corpora. We therefore propose a pragmatic "engineering" approach.

We have observed that the pattern of the first few head points varies substantially across corpora, and is difficult to model mathematically. Given this, and given the potential importance

---

[2]Note that Petersen et al. plot probability against word frequency rather than probability against rank.

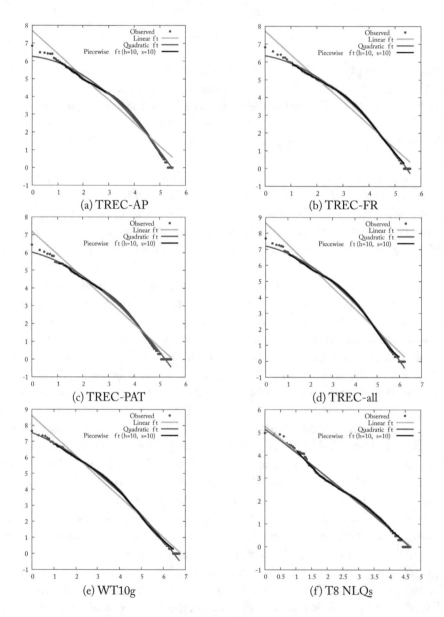

Figure 4.1: Word probability distributions in log-log space for our principal corpora. Lines of linear, quadratic, and piecewise linear fit are also shown. Note that in this and following figures, the piecewise fit covers only the middle section of the plot. In the piecewise model, the h head points and the singletons are explicitly modeled.

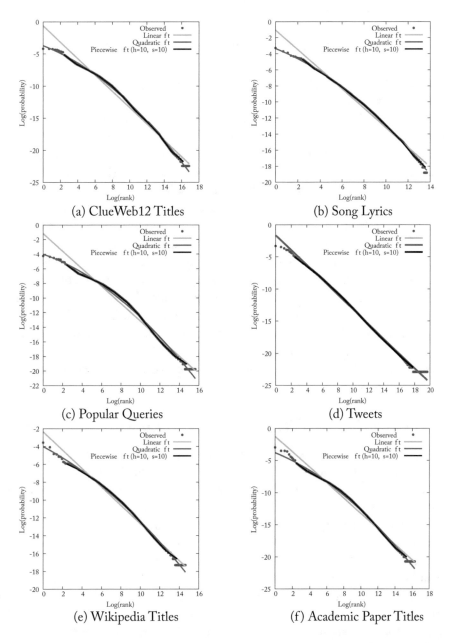

Figure 4.2: As for the previous figure but showing corpora comprising large numbers of very short texts: web page titles, song lyric lines, popular web queries, tweets, Wikipedia titles, and academic paper titles.

of the frequency of the most common words to indexing efficiency, we chose to record the actual probabilities of the first h words as parameters of the model. By inspection of the 11 corpora, we concluded that $h = 10$ would adequately cover the head deviations from linear or quadratic models. We have used $h = 10$ in our experiments but it could be that a smaller value would suffice, or a collection-dependent value would be better. Changing h would only slightly change the size and complexity of the model.

We also decided to model the singleton words separately. The relevant model parameter is w_1, the proportion of the vocabulary which has a frequency of one.

Finally, we chose to model the middle part of the curve using a piecewise linear model with s segments. The segment ends are equally spaced in the horizontal ($\log(rank)$) dimension. This model is mathematically simpler than the parabolic fractal model, and—given a large enough s—can accurately model departures from the quadratic fit. Each segment is described by a tuple of four values: first rank, last rank,[3] slope in log-log space, and sum of term probabilities within the domain of the segment. From inspection we were confident that ten segments would be sufficient to fit most corpora well enough. Accordingly, we chose $s = 10$. As with h, changing s would change the size and complexity of the model, but the effect would be small.

Table 4.2 shows all the parameters of our static model. For $h = 10$, $s = 10$ the size of the word frequency distribution model is 53 numeric quantities. That is five or six orders of magnitude smaller than a full language model. Note that when $s = 1$, $h = 0$, and $w_1 = 0$ the model reduces to a straightforward Zipfian one.

We assign word-ids $1 \ldots h$ to the head, $h + 1 \ldots m$ to the middle and $m + 1 \ldots |V|$ to the tail, where $m = |V| - w_1 \times |V|$.

4.3   WORD-ID SAMPLING: PRACTICAL MATTERS

The starting point for generation of integers representing word-ids is a uniform pseudo-random number generator. Selection of this primary random number generator is critical. It must have a very long period, have sufficient resolution to generate billions of distinct values, and be fast and memory-efficient.

The Mersenne Twister [61] algorithm has a reputation for fast generation of high-quality pseudorandom numbers. We chose to use the TinyMT64 version[4] to keep the memory footprint small. It has a period of $2^{127} - 1$ which is adequate for our purposes.

A double-precision random number R in $0 \ldots 1$ can be used to select head, middle, or tail fraction, based on H and $w_1 \times |V|/P$. If R falls into the head section, R is compared with each of the cumulative H_i values until the id of the correct head term is found and emitted. If R falls into the tail section, we simply emit the next word-id in sequence from a dedicated range of word-ids whose lowest value is determined from $|V|$, P, and w_1.

---

[3]The redundancy of recording the last rank of one segment and the first of the next could be avoided.
[4]http://www.math.sci.hiroshima-u.ac.jp/~m-mat/MT/TINYMT/index.html

Table 4.2: Parameters of our static corpus model

Parameter(s)	Explanation
N	Number of documents
P	Total of word occurrences
$|V|$	Vocabulary size
w_1	The proportion of distinct words which occur only once
h	The number of head points explicitly modeled
$H_1 \dots H_h$	The percentages of all word occurrences represented by each of the most frequent h words ($h \geq 0$)
s	The number of piecewise segments used to model the middle section ($s > 0$)
$S_1 \dots S_s$	The 4-tuples of the s segments used in piecewise linear approximation to the middle part of the curve
	Document–length distribution
	Word–length distribution
	Word representation method

For the remaining middle terms we select the appropriate piecewise segment by comparing R against the cumulative probabilities in S_i. We then transform R into the range $0 \dots 1$ and map it to a word-id by treating it as an area under the "Zipf" line represented by the segment and solving for the term rank, i.e., numerical word-id.

The integral with respect to rank r of the continuous Zipf function is

$$\int \frac{r^{\alpha+1}}{\alpha + 1} + c$$

for $\alpha \neq -1$. If the first and last ranks of the selected segment are f and l, respectively, then the area under the segment is given by:

$$A_{f \dots l} = \frac{l^{\alpha+1}}{\alpha + 1} - \frac{f^{\alpha+1}}{\alpha + 1}.$$

We want to scale up this area to 1, because R has been transformed into $0 \dots 1$. The scale factor is thus $F = 1/A_{f \dots l}$ and the scaled area under the curve from $r = 0$ to $r = f - 1$ is thus $A_{0-(f-1)} = F \times \frac{(f-1)^{\alpha+1}}{\alpha+1}$.

To assign a random number R to a word, we convert it to $R' = R + A_{0 \dots (f-1)}$ and solve $R' = F \times \frac{r^{\alpha+1}}{\alpha+1}$ for r. We then convert fractional r to the smallest integer t which is larger than

r:

$$t = \left\lceil \exp\left(\frac{\log(R' \times (\alpha + 1))}{\alpha + 1}\right) \right\rceil.$$

Once a word instance has been identified as "the word at rank t," we need to produce the character string corresponding to that term. Methods for doing that are discussed in Chapter 6.

Unfortunately, if we generate P word-ids from the three-part model described thus far, we will see vocabulary under-generation because we are still sampling with replacement. Our solution is described in the next section.

4.4   SAMPLING WORD-IDS WITHOUT REPLACEMENT

The mathematics in the previous section allows us to calculate the occurrence frequency of each of the words $1 \ldots |V|$. The frequency of a word corresponds to the area under the relevant piece-wise segment which corresponds to that word. Instead of randomly sampling from the distribution, we just calculate areas.

CORPUSGENERTOR allocates a word-id array T of dimension P, and instantiates all the occurrences of each of the terms into T. If the area under the relevant segment (assuming $h = 0$) for the highest frequency word tells us that it occurs f_1 times then we fill the first f_1 elements of T with 1, then append f_2 occurrences of 2 and so on until all P elements are filled.

Conversion of floating point numbers into integers inevitably results in an accumulation of error. It is necessary to adjust word frequencies slightly to ensure that the vocabulary size is exactly $|V|$ and that the total number of postings is exactly P.

We then use Durstenfeld's shuffle in combination with the TinyMT random number generator to randomly distribute the word occurrences within T. To generate the corpus, we insert document boundaries according to the document length distribution model. Then we read T in sequence, emitting the word representation corresponding to each term number encountered and emitting document boundaries where indicated.

4.5   EMULATION EXPERIMENTS ASSUMING WORD INDEPENDENCE

For many corpora we used either the SynthaCorpus `emulateARealCorpus.pl` script or one of the encryption or Markov generators to produce a synthetic emulated version. We present base vs. emulated comparisons in tables and figures.

Table 4.3 presents JSD values between the word frequency distributions of the emulated corpus relative to the base. Unsurprisingly, Caesar1 and Nomenclator show a perfect match. Despite the fact that vocabulary sizes are much smaller for the word-based Markov methods, the JSDs are very small—because the words missing from the emulated corpus have very low probability in the base. Modeling a corpus assuming uniform word probability performs very

Table 4.3: Emulation accuracy (JSD) of the word frequency distribution for a number of corpora and a number of emulation methods. The JS divergence between the emulated version of the corpus and the base version is calculated using the full distributions. Note that the word at rank r in the emulated corpus is matched with the word at rank r in the base, even if they are different words. The results for STRINGMARKGEN (abbreviated to stringMark. in the table) were obtained with $k = 13, \lambda = 0$. Divergences are reported for only a single run and, for most of the methods, would vary depending upon the random seed.

Emulation Methods	TREC-AP	TREC-FR	TREC-PAT	TREC-all	WT10g	T8 NLQs
CAESAR1	0.000	0.000	0.000	0.000	0.000	0.000
NOMEN.	0.000	0.000	0.000	0.000	0.000	0.000
GPT-2	0.005	0.011	0.034	—	—	0.008
WBMARKOV0	0.000	0.000	0.001	0.000	0.001	0.004
WBMARKOV1	0.000	0.000	0.001	0.000	0.001	0.007
STRINGMARK.	0.001	0.004	0.004	0.001	0.004	0.006
UNIFORM	0.819	0.845	0.831	0.898	0.889	0.643
LINEAR	0.308	0.296	0.249	0.300	0.300	0.232
PIECEWISE	0.000	0.000	0.000	0.000	0.000	0.003

badly. Most interestingly, Piecewise modeling performs very much better than Linear. Note that head words and singletons were not explicitly modeled in either the Uniform or Linear case.

Figure 4.3 presents comparisons of word frequency distributions for the case where emulation uses a three-part piecewise model. As may be seen, modeling is very accurate. In contrast, Figure 4.4 compares the distribution of significant bigrams[5] when the emulation assumes word independence. Modeling of bigram frequencies is very poor—the number of significant bigrams found in the emulated corpus is an order of magnitude less, and the frequency of the most frequent bigram is almost two orders of magnitude less. In the next chapter, we will attempt to close this gap by modeling n-grams.

4.5.1   MARKOV AND NEURAL METHODS

Our emulation of TREC-AP using GPT-2 resulted in a vocabulary size more than three times larger than that of the base. In contrast the vocabulary size resulting from WBMARKOV0 emulation of the same corpus produced a vocabulary 15% smaller. For WBMARKOV1 the vocabulary shrinkage (see page 8) was 14%, while for STRINGMARKOVGEN with $k = 23$ and no smoothing

---
[5]See Section 5.1 for an explanation of significance in this context.

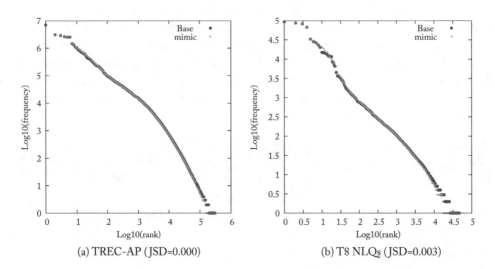

(a) TREC-AP (JSD=0.000)   (b) T8 NLQs (JSD=0.003)

Figure 4.3: Base vs. emulated word-frequency distributions in log-log space for a selection of the corpora. Word-frequency modeling was done using the three-part, piecewise model with $h = 10$, $s = 10$. Plots for TREC-FR, TREC-PAT, TREC-all, and WT10g show similarly accurate modeling, with JSD = 0.000 in each case.

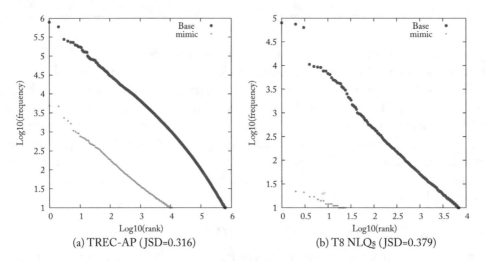

(a) TREC-AP (JSD=0.316)   (b) T8 NLQs (JSD=0.379)

Figure 4.4: Base vs. emulated bigram-frequency distributions in log-log space for the principal corpora. Word frequency modeling was done using the three-part, piecewise model with $h = 10$, $s = 10$. Plots for TREC-FR, TREC-PAT, TREC-all, and WT10g show similarly poor accuracy of modeling, with JSD > 0.2 in each case.

it was 16%. Note that addition of noise to the word-based Markov models does not solve the vocabulary shrinkage problem. It can generate previously unseen word sequences but cannot extend the "alphabet" of words.

Despite the fact that the implementations of word-based Markov and neural methods do a bad job of emulating the vocabulary size of a base corpus, Figure 4.5 shows that these methods do a very good job of emulating the shape of the ranked word frequency distribution.

String-based Markov generators are capable of solving the vocabulary shrinkage problem through appropriate choice of k (the number of characters of context used in choosing the next output character) and λ (the probability of choosing a lower order model when choosing the next output character in order to introduce noise).

Figure 4.6 shows the effect on vocabulary size of varying k. As expected, small values of k lead to over-generation of the vocabulary of $\mathbb{B}$ due to relatively unconstrained generation of word strings never seen in the language of the original corpus. With larger values of k and no noise, string generation is more constrained and we see vocabulary shrinkage.

A second line in Figure 4.6 shows the percentage of distinct words in $\mathbb{M}$ which were also present in $\mathbb{B}$. As expected, for values of k greater than about eight, the overlap is close to 100%. The third line in each plot shows the percentage of sentences in $\mathbb{M}$ which were present in $\mathbb{B}$. For these experiments we further pre-processed the two corpora to case-fold, remove all punctuation, and insert line breaks in place of ".", "!", "?". As can be seen there is a very high level of overlap for the T8 NLQs corpus (92.8% for $k = 23$), reflecting the relatively small amount of training data and the heavily repeated query forms, e.g., "where can i ...." The amount of sentence overlap for the sentence-split version of TREC-AP is only a very small percentage, but a nonetheless significant number. For $k = 23$ the percentage overlap is only 0.06% but there are 2184 overlapping sentences. This would potentially constitute a serious leak of confidential information. We will return to this issue in Chapter 11.

Figure 4.7 shows the same overlaps for the case where k is fixed at 23 but λ is varied. The w parameter is also fixed, at 21, meaning that when a reduced context is used the length of the context is $k - w = 2$. In the left-hand plot for T8 NLQs we see that $\lambda \geq 10^{-2.5}$ is able to overcome the tendency to under-generate the vocabulary and that overlaps of vocabulary and sentences decline at around the same point.

For the right-hand plot for TREC-AP much smaller values of λ, $\lambda \geq 10^{-6.5}$ achieve similar effects. Although not discernible from the graph, the percentage sentence overlap drops from 0.10–0.00.

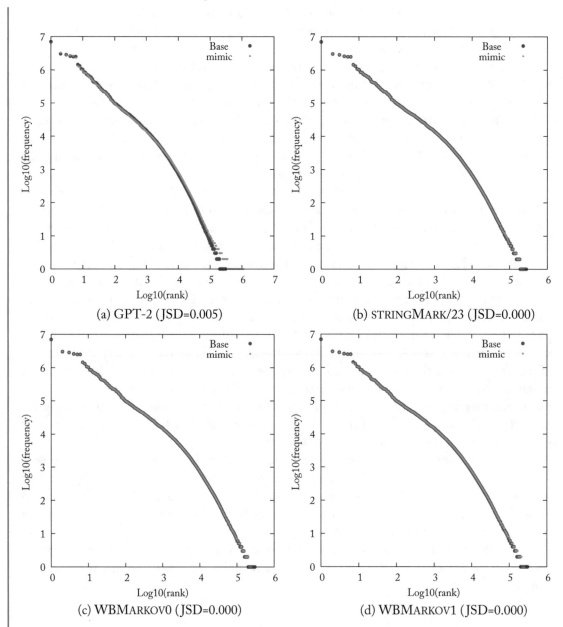

Figure 4.5: Fidelity of emulation of the word-frequency distributions for the TREC-AP corpus by neural and Markov methods. "stringMark/23" means STRINGMARKOVGEN with $k = 23, \lambda = 0$.

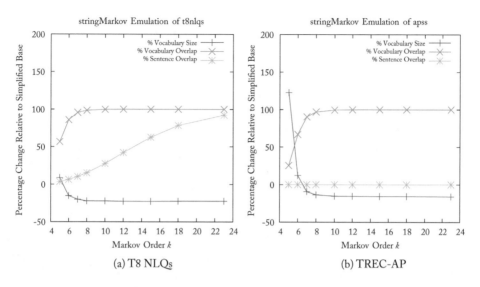

Figure 4.6: STRINGMARKOVGEN: The effect of k on vocabulary shrinkage, vocabulary overlap, and sentence overlap $\lambda = 0$.

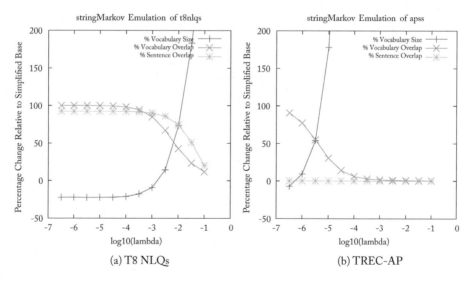

Figure 4.7: STRINGMARKOVGEN: $k = 23, w = 21$ The effect of λ on vocabulary shrinkage, vocabulary overlap, and sentence overlap.

CHAPTER 5

Modeling Term Dependence

Term dependence manifests itself as patterns of word associations which would be very unlikely to be observed if words were randomly scattered throughout the corpus.

For simplicity, our discussion of term dependence assumes that the documents in a corpus form an unordered set. This allows us to avoid considering possible term associations across document boundaries.

In a time-ordered corpus such as one from a newswire service such associations would be important, and essential to support a topic detection and tracking application. For example, the phrase "novel coronavirus" would rarely occur prior to December 2019, occur very frequently in documents from the next few months and then, hopefully, retreat to relative obscurity. However, modeling within-document term associations and generating corpora to match the model has proven quite challenging.

5.1 SIGNIFICANT WORD ASSOCIATIONS

If we were to repeatedly generate corpora using CORPUSGENERATOR and a term-independent model, we would observe a distribution of occurrence frequencies of the event of interest, e.g., an n-gram or a term co-occurrence relation. Since they occur by chance, such frequencies convey no additional information.

We can use the distribution of occurrence frequencies generated from an independence model to identify meaningful associations in a base corpus $\mathbb{B}$. Given a desired confidence level of say 95% we can then choose a criterion frequency CF such that 95% of the generated corpora would show an occurrence frequency less than CF. If we observe an occurrence frequency higher than CF in $\mathbb{B}$, then we conclude that there is a non-random association between the words participating in the relation.

Let us illustrate the procedure for calculating CF using a simple case, that of 2-grams.

The probability that word A will be followed by word B is essentially the product of the occurrence probabilities of the two words, calculated for A as $\Pr(A) = f_A/P$. Generating a corpus $\mathbb{M}$ containing P word occurrences and N documents by random scattering can be modeled as $U = P - N$ Bernoulli trials,[1] in which the probability of success is $p = \Pr AB = \Pr A \times \Pr B$. If the corpus were generated an infinite number of times then the number of occurrences of AB in $\mathbb{M}$ would form a binomial distribution (assuming replacement) or a hypergeometric distribution (without replacement). In either case we can approximate the distribution of numbers of

---

[1] $P - N$ because the last word in each document cannot be the start of a 2-grams.

occurrences of AB as a Gaussian with mean of $U \times p$ and variance of $U \times p(1 - p)$, because the number of trials can be assumed to be very large. In a Gaussian distribution, 95% of all observations fall below a z-score of $+1.65$, so we can set our criterion frequency as follows:

$$CF = U \times p + 1.65 \times \sqrt{U \times p \times (1 - p)}.$$

If AB occurs more than CF times we can say with 95% confidence that the words A and B are 2-gram dependent. We use a one-tailed test, because we're not considering negative associations, i.e., that AB occurs significantly less often than would be expected by chance. The criterion frequency can be based on a higher or lower Z score to control the balance between misses and false positives.

We call the relationships between words which occur more often than would be expected by chance, "significant." For example, "significant bigrams."

The above example can easily be extended to n-grams. (The number of Bernoulli trials must be reduced to $P - N \times (n - 1)$ since none of the $n - 1$ words at the end of each document can be the start of an n-gram.)

We note that dependence may occur between words (primary dependence) or between higher-order terms such as phrases, proximities, or co-occurrences (secondary dependence), but our current project considers only primary dependences, of which we identify three types:

Word co-occurrence — This is the tendency of certain sets of words to occur together. For example, the words "politician" may commonly co-occur with "vote," "party," "parliament," etc. When counting co-occurrences between word A and B, one may just count the number of documents in which words A and B co-occur and model repetitions of the co-occurrence relation as a secondary dependence. Alternatively, we can count the number of co-occurrences within a document as $\min(tf(A), tf(B))$. Computing co-occurrence relations is potentially very expensive computationally though faster algorithms have recently become available [12]. Computational complexity rises when the degree of the co-occurrence relation is increased, e.g., A co-occurs with B and with C.

Word burstiness or self co-occurrence — this is the tendency of the occurrences of a word (usually a content-bearing rather than a functional word) to cluster into fewer documents than would be expected with random scatter. For example a document about the economy may contain many more occurrences of "unemployment" than would be expected by chance. If term A is bursty, then we would observe that the distribution of $tf(A)$ values would deviate substantially from what would be expected from random scatter and consequently the word would occur in significantly fewer documents than would be expected under random scatter.

n-**grams** — This is a specific form of co-occurrence where the co-occurring words appear adjacent to each other and in sequence. Counting n-grams for small values of n is quite feasible

Table 5.1: Co-occurrence relation: Calculating the criterion frequencies for various pairs of df values in a corpus of 250,000 documents. The method is the same as that given in the text for 2-grams except that the joint probability p is calculated from dfs, and the number of Bernoulli trials is N.

df_A	$Pr(A)$	df_B	$Pr(B)$	P	N	$N \times p$	$N \times p \times (1-p)$	Crit. Freq.
1	4e–06	1,000	0.004	1.6e–08	250,000	0.004	0.0632	1
10	4e–05	1,000	0.004	1.6e–07	250,000	0.04	0.2000	1
100	0.0004	1,000	0.004	1.6e–06	250,000	0.4	0.6325	2
1,000	0.004	1,000	0.004	1.6e–05	250,000	4	2.0000	8
10,000	0.04	1,000	0.004	0.00016	250,000	40	6.3240	51
100,000	0.4	1,000	0.004	0.0016	250,000	400	19.9840	433
100,000	0.4	100	0.0004	0.00016	250,000	40	6.3240	51
100,000	0.4	10	4e–05	1.6e–05	250,000	4	2.0000	8
100,000	0.4	1	4e–06	1.6e–06	250,000	0.4	0.6325	2

computationally but there are complications due to overlap and subsumption. For example, "great barrier reef marine park authority" is a 6-gram which subsumes many n-grams of lesser degree, such as "great barrier reef" and "barrier reef marine park." In this example the subsumed n-grams overlap.

Determining significance for co-occurrences is potentially much more complicated because documents vary substantially in length. Baeza-Yates and Navarro [6] discuss this and provide a formula for calculating the probability of finding a word k times in a document containing w words, where the word occurs f times in a corpus of P word occurrences.

However, we believe that a rough approximation will be good enough and assume that documents are of uniform length. We know df_A, the number of documents containing at least one occurrence of word A. The probability that an instance of A will occur in document d_i can be modeled as $\frac{df_A}{N}$. Therefore, the joint probability of an instance of A and an instance of B occurring in the same document is given by:

$$p = \frac{df_A \times df_B}{N^2}$$

and the number of Bernoulli trials is N.

Table 5.1 gives some example CF values for different values of p_1 and p_2. If for example we found that mad with $df = 1000$ and meataxe with $df = 1000$ co-occurred 9 times we would conclude that mad and meataxe exhibited a dependence, because the criterion is 8.

SYNTHACORPUS represents r-fold repetition of a word in a document as the word followed by an "@" and the value of r. For example, `walrus@5` signifies the word "walrus" appearing exactly 5 times in a document. By treating `walrus@r` as an r-way self co-occurrence, we can estimate its expected probability of occurrence as:

$$p = \left(\frac{df_{\texttt{walrus}}}{N} \right)^r$$

and use the same method to calculate criterion frequencies. Again, the number of Bernoulli trials is N.

In corpora where document lengths vary considerably—that's most of them—the calculation of random-scatter expected co-occurrence frequencies based on dfs stretches credibility.

It is also possible that certain pairs of words may exhibit a negative dependence, i.e., that the words co-occur significantly less often than would be expected under random scatter. This could obviously occur in a corpus comprising a mixture of documents in English and documents in French. In such a corpus, "le" and "the" would likely co-occur less frequently than would be expected. Explicit modeling of negative dependence is beyond the scope of the present work.

In previous sections we have described our implementation of a system capable of achieving very accurate emulation of the properties of a corpus, excluding term dependence properties. We would now like to extend the model to include at least primary term dependence. Before attempting this, we discuss the capabilities of Markov and neural models.

5.2   WORD ASSOCIATIONS THROUGH MARKOV MODELING

A word-based Markov model of order 1 should result in good modeling of 2-grams because the transition table explicitly models the probabilities of word pairs. For example, the probability is much higher that "weather" will be followed by "forecast" or "map" than by "green."

Figure 5.1 confirms that this is the case. Figure 5.2 shows that modeling of 3-grams is also quite good, while modeling of the tendency of words to occur in bursts is relatively poor.

Higher-order Markov models should do a good job of modeling higher order n-grams. However, each increase in the order of the model causes a major jump in the size of the transition matrix, even when represented sparsely.

Experiments with STRINGMARKOVGEN, with $k = 23$ on TREC-AP show near perfect emulation of 2-grams (JSD = 0.002) and 2-, 3-grams frequencies (0.005). Emulation of word repetitions shows a slight improvement (JSD = 0.048) over the graph shown in Figure 5.2.

Whatever the order of the matrix, it is unlikely that Markov methods will successfully model word burstiness or word co-occurrence.

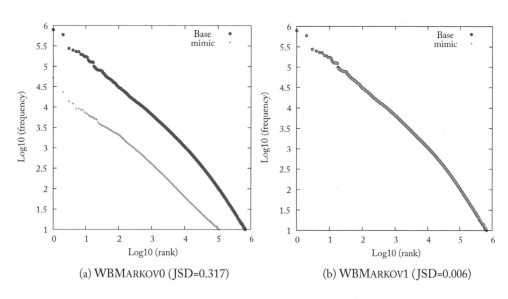

(a) WBMARKOV0 (JSD=0.317)   (b) WBMARKOV1 (JSD=0.006)

Figure 5.1: Comparing the frequency of 2-grams in WBMarkov0 and WBMarkov1 emulations of the TREC-AP corpus.

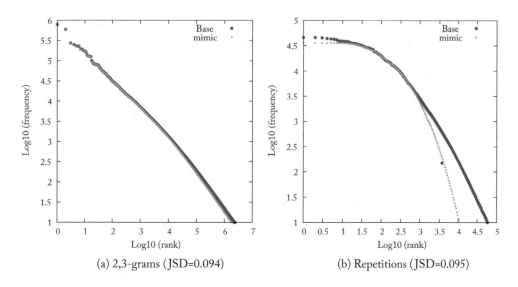

(a) 2,3-grams (JSD=0.094)   (b) Repetitions (JSD=0.095)

Figure 5.2: Comparing the fidelity of other inter-word relationships for the WBMarkov1 emulation of the TREC-AP corpus.

5.3   WORD ASSOCIATIONS THROUGH NEURAL MODELING

Various forms of deep learning systems specialize in learning sequences. They are potentially able to model longer n-grams and possibly word co-occurrences. It is less likely that they can model burstiness.

As noted elsewhere, we used GPT-2 to emulate the TREC-AP corpus. Figure 5.3 shows the effect of this emulation run on the generation of unigrams, bigrams, trigrams, and word bursts. Visually, emulation of unigrams and bigrams is near perfect, trigrams quite good, and word repetitions relatively poor.

5.4   REFINING CORPUSGENERATOR TO HANDLE DEPENDENCE

The algorithm described in Section 4.4 isn't compatible with term dependence because word-ids are generated independently and because shuffling occurs across document boundaries. Let us modify the algorithm to make it more compatible with dependence models.

As before, we generate a vocabulary, then use a term frequency model to generate a total occurrence frequency for each word in the vocabulary. Next, we use a document length model to generate a document table, and an array T with an element for each word occurrence. Entries in the document table include a pointer to the spot in T where the next word-id generated for this document should be placed, plus a count of free spots remaining for this document. We also mark the document ends in T. Then, in order of decreasing frequency, we consider each word and randomly scatter its occurrences across documents, inserting that word's id into the next available slot in T for that document. If the chosen document is already full then we choose again.[2]

Once all word occurrences have been placed, we randomly shuffle the words within each document. Finally, we emit word representations and document boundaries as per the original algorithm.

This refined algorithm can be more easily modified to handle term dependence. We generate the term dependences before individual words to reduce the chance that the chosen document will already be full. To illustrate the basic idea of the process, if our model tells us that words A and B co-occur 500 times then we first allocate 500 AB pairs to randomly chosen non-full documents and reduce the word frequencies of A and B by 500.

Let us consider the three types of association between words in the order: burstiness, n-grams, co-occurrences. Initially, we will consider each type of association independently, and then we will discuss the complexities of combining them.

---

[2]In practice, we use a much more efficient method. As documents fill up, we swap them to one end of the document table and make our choices within the non-full section. For allocations of single words this avoids the need for re-tries.

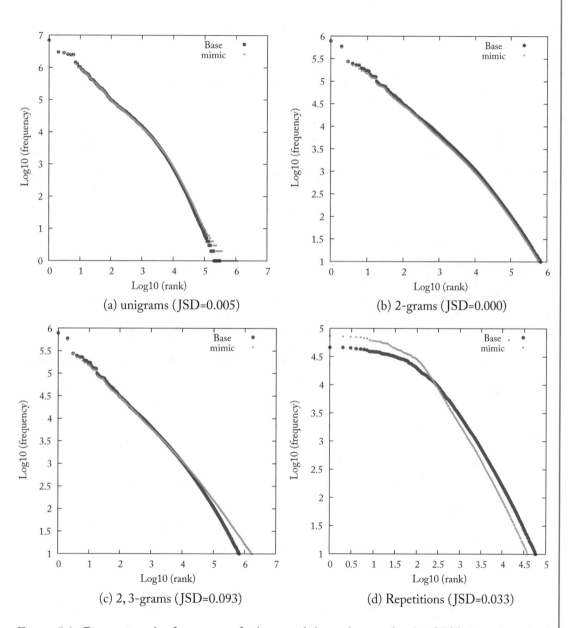

Figure 5.3: Comparing the frequency of other word dependencies for the GPT-2 emulation of the TREC-AP corpus.

5.5   WORD "BURSTINESS"

We can easily extract how many times a word occurs within a document in $\mathbb{B}$. Let us represent a term such as "bank," which occurs exactly k times ($k > 1$) in a document as "bank@k," and record counts of "bank@5," "bank@4," "bank@3," and "bank@2." To facilitate transfer to the emulated corpus $\mathbb{M}$ we would represent "bank" by its rank in the base word frequency distribution, e.g., "276@4."

Of course, frequent words will occur multiple times in some documents even under random scattering. We can use the overall probability of occurrence of a word such as word 276 to estimate how many documents are likely to contain k occurrences of it under random scatter.[3] If the observed count is much higher than the expected count, we call "276@k" a "k-burst."

To implement word burstiness in our corpus emulation system we first generate k-bursts then unigrams, after subtracting the word occurrences due to k-bursts from the unigram frequency. For example, if "276@5" occurs 100 times and the overall occurrence frequency of word 276 is 1000, then we distribute the 5-bursts across 100 documents and subtract 100×5 from the unigram frequency of word 276. Note that the k is an exact count, meaning that there is no overlap between 4-bursts and 5-bursts for the same term.

Initially, this approach results in all the terms in a burst occurring sequentially near the beginning of the document, but that is corrected by the within-document shuffling.

Modeling k-bursts complicates and slows down corpus emulation in two ways.

1. Retries may be necessary to find a document with sufficient room to accommodate a burst.

2. To achieve perfection, every allocation of words involved in a burst requires a check that the chosen document hasn't already been chosen for this term, e.g., if document d is chosen to receive a burst of 5 occurrences, then a subsequent allocation of the same word will convert the 5-burst to a 6-burst. Preventing this incurs significant extra cost, not only in determining whether this document already has occurrences of a burst of the word to be assigned, but also due to the need for the retries required when it has.

When assigning a k-burst to a document, we should adjust probabilities to take into account the length of the document. It would look strange to allocate seven occurrences of a word, say "electroplating," to a document with only seven words.

5.6 n-GRAMS

Let us consider using a variant of the k-burst mechanism described above for modeling n-gram dependence.

Let us assume that we are given a list of significant n-grams represented as a file in which each line is in a format exemplified by the following:

---

[3]Widely differing document lengths make it difficult to calculate this precisely.

```
(97,41,30012):57 -- "new south wales"
```

where the numbers in the parenthesized, comma-separated list are the base corpus ranks of the participating words, and the number after the colon records the total occurrence frequency of this 3-gram. The rest of the line shows the actual words and is for explanatory purposes only.

With n-grams, the algorithm for within-document shuffling must be modified to preserve the n-grams. We enable this by marking the first word in a generated n-gram with a head-of-n-gram flag, and each subsequent word with a tail-of-n-gram flag.

Let us consider the simplest case first, that of 2-grams. Even there, we see problems due to overlap.

5.6.1   2-GRAMS

If we find only two significant 2-grams: AB and CD, each occurring 100 times, then we can scatter those occurrences in similar fashion to k-bursts, subtracting 100 from the frequency of each of A, B, C, and D.

This approach seems straight-forward enough until we consider potentially overlapping 2-grams, e.g., AB and BC. When we look only at 2-grams, we don't know whether some of the ABs and BCs are actually part of a 3-gram ABC. Table 5.2 illustrates three different overlap cases. In the "No overlap" case there is no problem. In the "Overlap (1) case," our algorithm generates the correct counts for both unigrams and 2-grams and we are happy because we don't care about 3-grams. A difficulty arises in the "Overlap (2)" case because, while generating the BC occurrences the unigram count for B hits zero. "Overlap (2A)" shows the result of stopping the 2-gram generation at that point—we generate too few instances of "B C" but the correct number of Bs. "Overlap (2B)" shows the result of continuing to generate the specified number of BCs—we overgenerate Bs. Approach 2A seems superior because we consider it more important to maintain the correct unigram frequencies and the overall word occurrence count than the 2-gram counts.

5.6.2   EXTENDING TO HIGHER ORDER n-GRAMS

At the beginning of Section 5.6, the representation of a list of significant n-grams was described. We propose a generation algorithm (Algorithm 5.1) which relies on this list and also on an array, sorted by ascending word rank, of individual word frequencies. Let us now consider some specific higher-order cases.

If we consider 3-grams and unigrams but ignore 2-grams then we can take the same approach as for 2-grams in the previous section:

- Generate all $f(ABC)$ occurrences of ABC while subtracting $f(ABC)$ from the frequencies of A, B, and C.

Table 5.2: Contrived example illustrating the three main cases when generating 2-grams. A, B, and C represent distinct words. ABC represents the 3-grams comprising those three words in sequence. Entries in the table show the frequencies for each feature in $\mathbb{B}$ and the generated frequencies in $\mathbb{M}$. A question mark indicates that the frequency may vary depending upon the random generator. The "No overlap" and "Overlap (1)" cases are straightforward. In the "Overlap (2)" cases, approaches "(2A)" and "(2B)" show that it is necessary to choose between two imperfect outcomes.

	Base Corpus					Emulated Corpus				
	ABC	AB	BC	B Alone	Total B	ABC	AB	BC	B Alone	Total B
No overlap	0	100	100	0	200	?	100✓	100✓	0✓	200✓
Overlap (1)	50	100	100	100	250	?	100✓	100✓	50✓	250✓
Overlap (2A)	50	100	100	0	150	?	100✓	50✗	0✓	150✓
Overlap (2B)	50	100	100	0	150	?	100✓	100✓	0✓	200✗

- Do the corresponding thing for BCD and CDE but halt the process as soon as one of the unigram frequencies hits zero. (This gives priority to achieving accurate unigram counts and overall total term occurrence count.)

If we consider the 2-grams as well, each 3-gram ABC may have two subsumed 2-grams AB and BC. Note, it is possible that one or both of the subsumed 2-grams may not have been determined to be significant and may be missing from the list. Algorithm 5.1 should work in either case.

- Generate all $f(ABC)$ occurrences of ABC while subtracting $f(ABC)$ from the frequencies of AB and BC, assuming they have been noted as significant. Also subtract $f(ABC)$ from the frequencies of A, B, and C.

- Do the corresponding thing for BCD and CDE and their subsumed 2-grams, but halting the process as soon as one of the 2-gram or the unigram frequencies hits zero. (This gives priority to achieving accurate unigram counts and overall total term occurrence count.)

5.7 CO-OCCURRENCES

If we have a file of co-occurrences containing lines in the same format as for n-grams, e.g.,

```
(207,4101,300):117 -- economy, employment, finance
```

Algorithm 5.1 A general algorithm for n-gram generation. The test for exhaustion of a subsumed item actually needs to be more sophisticated than shown, because an n-gram may contain repeated elements, e.g., "dance dance revolution"

1: Sort the n-gram list, first by degree (numeric descending), then by each of component word positions from left to right (numeric ascending).
2: **for each** n-gram N in the list **do**
3:     $n \leftarrow$ cardinality of N
4:     FINISHED $\leftarrow$ **false**
5:     Extract the frequency $f(N)$ of N
6:     Compute S the set of all k-grams ($k < n$) and words subsumed by N
7:     **for** $f \leftarrow f(N)$ **down to** 1 **do**
8:         **for each** element S_i of S **do**
9:             **if** frequency of S_i is zero **then**
10:                 FINISHED $\leftarrow$ **true**
11:                 **break**
12:         **if** FINISHED **then**
13:             **break**
14:         **else**
15:             **for each** element S_i of S **do**
16:                 Decrement the frequency of S_i
17:             Randomly place an instance of N

---

then we can treat n-way co-occurrences in exactly the same way as n-grams, except that we don't need to use flags, because there is no need to preserve word order when internally shuffling.

An efficient algorithm for finding word co-occurrences due to Billerbeck et al. [12] requires the use of an inverted file. It is thus unlikely that this algorithm would be built into CORPUSPROPERTYEXTRACTOR.

5.8 SIMULTANEOUSLY MODELING BURSTINESS, n-GRAMS, AND CO-OCCURRENCES

Simultaneously modeling n-grams and co-occurrences could be approached as follows. We generate the n-grams first and for every n-gram instance generated (including subsumed n-grams) we decrement the frequency of the corresponding co-occurrence and its subsumed co-occurrences, if those co-occurrences are in the list. The 3-gram "new south wales" corresponds to a co-occurrence of new, south, and wales, which subsumes co-occurrences of: new, south; south, wales; and new, wales. Accordingly when we generate an instance of "new south wales" we must decrement the frequencies of each of those four co-occurrences, checking for zero frequencies.

When modeling k-bursts, we in any case have to check that a document chosen to receive a k-burst of term X_i doesn't already have occurrences of X_i. This check allows us to combine k-burst modeling with modeling n-grams and co-occurrences, provided that the k-bursts are generated last.

The order of generation would thus be:

1. n-grams

2. co-occurrences

3. k-bursts

4. individual words

Implementing this successfully will pose many challenges. Although a successful implementation may be expected to achieve a substantial step up in realism, we recognize that significant limitations remain on fidelity.

5.9   STATUS OF IMPLEMENTATION IN SYNTHACORPUS

The version of SynthaCorpus which was current at the time of writing (July 2020) implements n-grams up to at least $N = 5$, but doesn't yet implement co-occurrences, or k-bursts.

5.10   EMULATION WITH WORD DEPENDENCE MODELING

Graphs in Figure 4.4 on page 42 confirm that the assumption of word independence yields very poor modeling of 2-gram frequencies. Graphs in Figure 5.4 show that when 2-grams are explicitly modeled by CORPUSGENERATOR, the gap is substantially closed. However, careful examination of the head part of the graphs on the right reveals that there remains a gap.

The explanation is the problem of n-gram overlap, discussed in Section 5.6.1. Let us take as a real example the common 2-gram "find information" which occurs 10,575 times in the T8 NLQs corpus. There are two very common 2-grams starting with "information"—"information about" which occurs 4251 times, and "information on" which occurs 7668 times. The total occurrence frequency of "information" is 12,915. Say we generate the "find information" 2-grams first, reducing the number of singleton "information" instances still to be generated to $12,915 - 10,575 = 2340$. Then we attempt to generate the "information about" 2-grams, but after we have emitted 2340 of them, we notice that we have already generated all of the required occurrences of "information" and we must stop. As a result, we emit less than half of the required number of instances of "information about" 2-grams and none at all of the "information on" 2-grams.

Of course 2-gram overlap also occurs at the other end too—"i find" occurs 63,448 times, potentially causing even more under-generation.

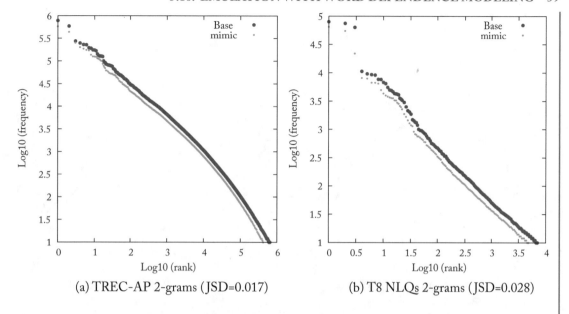

(a) TREC-AP 2-grams (JSD=0.017)   (b) T8 NLQs 2-grams (JSD=0.028)

Figure 5.4: CORPUSGENERATOR: Bigram frequency distributions in log-log space for two corpora. Note that in this figure, for both base and emulated corpora, only bigrams which occur more frequently than would be expected in a random scatter model are considered. Each graph plots bigram frequencies observed in the relevant corpus (base or emulated) and selected using identical decision criteria. Plots for TREC-FR, TREC-PAT, TREC-all, and WT10g show similarly accurate modeling, with JSD values ranging from 0.011–0.023. See Figure 4.4 for the corresponding plots generated assuming word independence.

Another effect of n-gram overlap is that the total number of postings which would be generated by n-grams is greater than the total number of postings required. To reduce this effect, we imposed more stringent thresholds on n-gram acceptance, e.g., for T8 NLQs that an n-gram should occur at least 10 times and achieve a frequency 10 standard deviations higher than expected by random scatter. In case this wasn't successful in all cases, we also introduced a heuristic in CORPUSGENERATOR—if the total number of postings specified by the n-grams is greater than 90% of the total number of postings to be generated for the corpus, we scale back the n-gram frequencies so that the total just reaches the 90% level. The actual number of postings generated will be much less than that due to the overlap issues we have been discussing.

Can we solve the overlap problem by recording and modeling higher-order n-grams? The answer is no, because there is still overlap. Figure 5.6 shows the result of modeling up to 5-grams. If we start with the 5-grams and generate 9944 occurrences of "where can i find information," we reduce the frequency of the subsumed 4-gram "can i find information" to 113. Then when

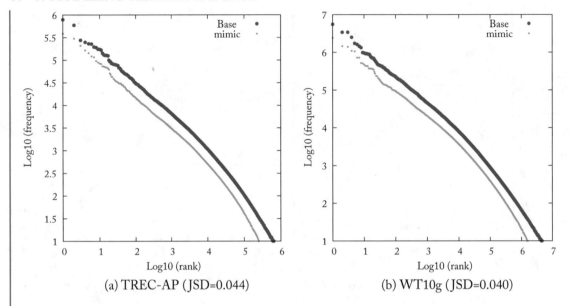

(a) TREC-AP (JSD=0.044)   (b) WT10g (JSD=0.040)

Figure 5.5: corpusGenerator: 2-gram frequency distributions in log-log space. Exploring the effect of modeling both 2-grams and 3-grams.

we try to emit "can i find information on" or "can i find information about," we dramatically under-generate because the frequency of the subsumed phrases soon reaches zero.

Disappointingly, Figure 5.5 shows that when both 2-grams and 3-grams are generated using the present algorithm, the frequency distribution of 2-grams is less accurately modeled.

5.11   DISCUSSION AND STATUS

Even though we have not yet attempted to modify corpusGenerator to handle any types of dependency other than n-grams, difficulties are already apparent. Serious problems arise because of n-gram overlap. When generating high-order n-grams, we decrement the frequency of subsumed lower-order grams and single words. Quite often that results in frequencies declining to zero, falsely implying that individual words never appear by themselves.

A better method for extracting significant n-grams is needed which better takes into account overlap. That, along with modeling of other forms of dependency remains for future work. We hope that readers will tackle this interesting and challenging problem. Perhaps the best hope for modeling n-gram dependence in an emulated or scaled-up corpus lies in a Markov or neural model.

However, the "Repetitions" plots in Figures 5.2 and 5.3 suggest that neither the Markov models nor GPT-2 are able to faithfully model word burstiness. Since burstiness is effectively self-co-occurrence, we suspect that these models would also fail to adequately model

```
10575 -- "find information"
10423 -- "i find information"
10057 -- "can i find information"
9944 -- "where can i find information"
6572 -- "find information on"
6508 -- "i find information on"
6250 -- "can i find information on"
3768 -- "find information about"
3694 -- "i find information about"
3596 -- "can i find information about"
1232 -- "find information on the"
1222 -- "i find information on the"
635 -- "find information about the"
622 -- "i find information about the"
256 -- "do i find information"
197 -- "where do i find information"
182 -- "do i find information on"
```

Figure 5.6: *n*-grams up to $n = 5$ extracted from T8 NLQs which contain "find information."

co-occurrence. An approach to modeling burstiness in CORPUSGENERATOR is presented in Section 5.5. Although there are complications, an implementation would not have to deal with the problems of overlap and subsumption which affect *n*-grams. Given a list of co-occurrence relations, generating co-occurrences in CORPUSGENERATOR may also be feasible.[4]

For simulating retrieval system performance—both indexing and bag-of-words query processing—it is likely to be more important to accurately model term burstiness and co-occurrence than to accurately model *n*-grams.

---

[4]See Section 5.7.

CHAPTER 6

Modeling Word Strings

The SYNTHACORPUS methods for generating words (Chapters 4 and 5) are concerned with generating a series of integers R_i representing the ranks of the words in a Zipf-style ordering. If we are given a lexicon (for example the lexicon of a corpus being emulated), we can convert each R_i to a string by simple look-up. If we have no lexicon and no interest in the actual textual representations, we can emit strings such as "t27," representing the 27th most frequently occurring word.

However, in many simulation scenarios, we need to generate word strings from the word-ids output from the word generator. This is self-evidently the case when scaling up a corpus, or when engineering a totally artificial one, or to more carefully preserve confidentiality of a corpus. The choice of the strings for the words may also be important in efficiency experimentation. The choice has a practical effect on:

1. the size in bytes of the corpus;

2. the compressibility of the corpus text; and

3. the performance of the vocabulary structure used by an indexer, such as the collision rate of a hashing method, or the balance of a tree.

In this chapter we study the characteristics of word strings in English and discuss methods for generating them. We regret that time and space do not permit us to extend our study to other languages.

Please note that when discussing frequencies we sometimes aggregate over the distinct words in a vocabulary, and sometimes over all word occurrences in a corpus. We try to always make it clear which method we are using.

6.1 DISTRIBUTION OF LETTER AND LETTER PAIR FREQUENCIES

It's possible that distributions of letters and letter pairs may affect certain data structures such as tries and suffix arrays. For completeness we study and compare distributions.

Letter frequency histograms can be compiled in four different ways, depending upon whether the letters are counted across the distinct words in the vocabulary or the word occurrences in the corpus, and whether the horizontal axis of the histogram is ordered alphabetically or in order of decreasing frequency. We use only the frequency ordered form.

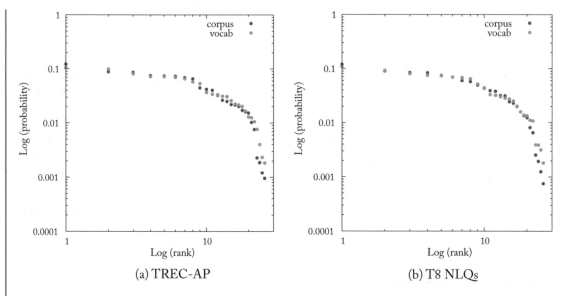

Figure 6.1: Distributions of letter probabilities, derived by counting in two ways. First is by counting across all word occurrences in the corpus. Second is by counting across distinct words in the vocabulary. Plots for TREC-FR, TREC-PAT, TREC-all, and WT10g show similar patterns.

Figure 6.1 presents the ranked distributions obtained in each of the two ways of counting for a two of the corpora we are using. The graphs show little difference between the two ways of counting except that the rarest letters have lower probabilities in the corpus than among the distinct words. It is clear that none of the distributions are well modeled by a Zipf distribution.

Figure 6.2 shows the ranked distribution of letter pair frequencies in the same two corpora. None of these distributions are well modeled by a Zipf distribution, either.

6.2   DISTRIBUTION OF WORD LENGTHS

Figure 6.3 shows the distributions of word lengths for words in the lexicons of six corpora. It can be seen that some of these distributions closely approximate a normal distribution and that others deviate far from normality. In five out of the six cases, the mode of the fitted normal[1] corresponds very closely to the mode of the real distribution. The exception is TREC-all whose multiple modes likely arise from the fact that it is an aggregation of sub-corpora from different sources.

For all six corpora, the mean length of distinct words lies between 6.5 and 8.1 letters. It seems intuitive that the mean length should correspond to a word of medium length, since

---

[1]In a normal distribution, mode, median, and mean coincide.

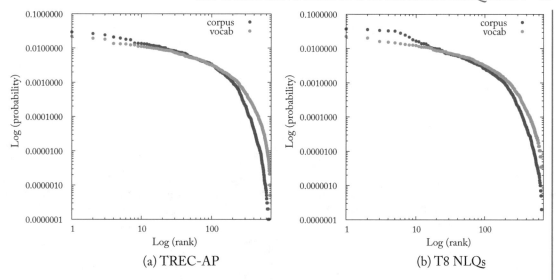

(a) TREC-AP   (b) T8 NLQs

Figure 6.2: Distributions of letter pair probabilities, derived by counting in two ways. First is by counting across all word occurrences in the corpus. Second is by counting across distinct words in the vocabulary. Plots for TREC-FR, TREC-PAT, TREC-all, and WT10g show similar patterns.

the number of pronounceable short sequences of letters is quite limited, and there is a bias in English against very long words.

The reason why the means of the length distributions for distinct words and for word occurrences differ substantially (for TREC-AP the values are 7.50 and 4.78) is the tendency for commonly occurring words to be short.

6.3   WORD LENGTH AND OCCURRENCE FREQUENCY

It is well established [80, 92] that there is a relationship between word length and word frequency: frequently occurring words tend to be shorter. Unfortunately, there is no simple function to map a word's rank to its length.

We confirmed this relationship on our six corpora by plotting the mean and standard deviation of the distribution of occurrence frequencies for all the words of each length. These are shown in Figure 6.4. The asymetry of the standard deviation "whiskers" is due to the log scale used on the vertical axis.

Table 6.1 presents in a different way the relationship between word occurrence frequency (actually rank in the ordered list of frequencies) and word length for the very large vocabulary of the ClueWeb12 corpus.[2] We divided the vocabulary into logarithmically sized buckets and

---

[2]http://www.lemurproject.org/clueweb12.php/

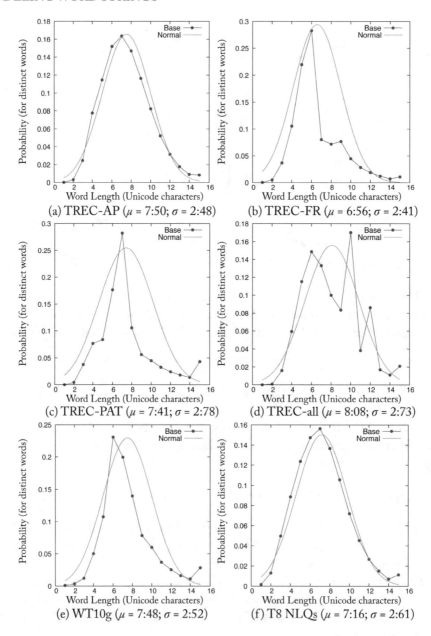

Figure 6.3: Distributions of the lengths of distinct words in the lexicons of several corpora, with a corresponding normal curve. Note that the means and standard deviations refer to the distributions for distinct words. The means of the distributions for word occurrences are generally much smaller.

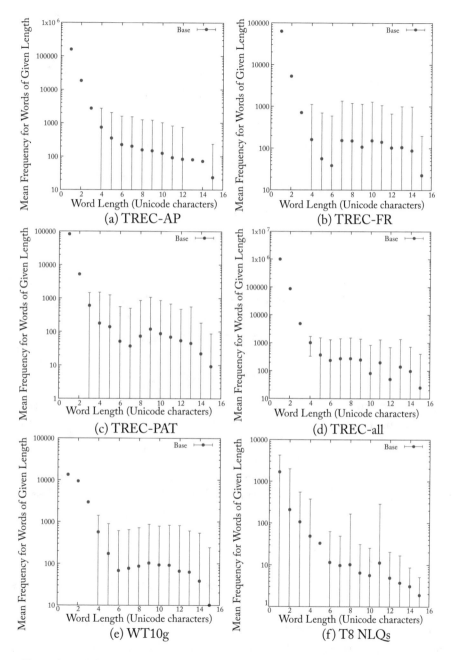

Figure 6.4: Distributions of the occurrence frequencies for words of a given length. Points show the mean frequency and bars indicate the standard deviation of the distribution of frequencies.

Table 6.1: Means and standard deviations of lengths of words in ClueWeb12 based on word ranks grouped into log10 buckets. There were a total of approximately 89 million words.

Bucket	Rank Range	Mean Length	Standard Deviation
0	1–9	2.222	0.629
1	10–99	3.844	1.831
2	100–999	5.600	2.123
3	1,000–9,999	6.744	2.425
4	10,000–99,999	7.204	2.586
5	100,000–999,999	8.265	2.759
6	1,000,000–9,999,999	9.415	2.802
7	10,000,000–99,999,999	9.736	2.568

calculated the mean and standard deviation of the lengths in each bucket. As may be seen, the mean word length increases with the bucket number. The variability in the lengths also increases up to the second last bucket. Note that the last bucket is not completely full.

Sigurd et al. [80] modeled the distribution of word lengths in English and Swedish using the formula:

$$f_{\exp} = a \times L^b \times c^L,$$

where $f_{\exp}$ is the expected total frequency of words of length L, and a, b, and c are empirically determined constants, $0 < c < 1$. Sigurd et al. note that this formula corresponds to a Gamma distribution.

Unfortunately, a model of the combined frequency of words of a particular length helps little in modeling how many letters there should be in the string representing a particular word W_i (identified by its rank R_i in the word frequency distribution), and helps even less in modeling what those letters should be. We therefore seek a word string generator with the following characteristics.

One-to-one Each word rank R_i should map to a different simulated word.

Word length The distribution of word lengths should approximate that expected for a real corpus.

Letter frequency Word strings should have an appropriate distribution of letters.

Data structure stress Ideally, the synthesized lexicon should stress vocabulary structures, such as trees, tries, suffix arrays, or hash tables to a similar extent to that of a real corpus. This is difficult to assess in general, but can be tested with reference to a specific implementation.

Resource usage Ideally, the method should be fast and memory efficient.

Table 6.2: The first eight rows of the Base26s multiplier table for the real ClueWeb12 data. Base26s uses the relationship between word length and S_L to achieve a realistic distribution of word lengths. In practice this table would need to be extracted for the specific corpus being emulated.

Word Length	Cumulative Frequency	S_L
1	26	1
2	702	1
3	18,278	1
4	449,647	1
5	3,082,702	5
6	9,621,775	47
7	19,857,953	785
8	32,701,943	16,259

6.4   METHODS FOR GENERATING WORD STRINGS

Methods for generating artificial words include various forms of hashing into a restricted alphabet, as well as more complex methods explored recently by Sutskever et al. [83] and the Markovian models pioneered by Shannon [79].

Let us consider a range of models for generating the text of words in a simulated corpus. Models vary in complexity, memory requirements, degree of fidelity, amount of training data needed, and speed of generation.

Base26   A fast, very simple method for generating words from an alphabet $\mathbb{A}$ is to represent the rank R as a number in base $\mathbb{A}$ using letters of the alphabet as digits. With a lowercase English alphabet ($|\mathbb{A}| = 26$) the first 26 ranks are all the 1-letter words, then the next $26^2 = 676$ are all the 2-letter words, and so on. Unfortunately, using this approach, we cannot expect a realistic distribution of letters or of word lengths. A variant called Base26s is proposed to achieve a more realistic distribution of word lengths.

Base26s   This approach rests on the observation that the sparsity of words of a particular length increases with the length, as illustrated in Table 6.2. Note that when emulating a corpus $\mathbb{B}$, we should use a sparsity table generated from $\mathbb{B}$'s vocabulary.

We estimate the average "skip" S_L between successive words of length L, as the ratio of the number of possible words of length L (i.e., $|\mathbb{A}|^L$) to the number of observed words of that length. We then calculate $R'_i = S_L \times R_i$ and express R'_i in base $|\mathbb{A}|$. Provided that S_L increases monotonically with L, there is no possibility that a word will be generated more than once, and the only additional memory requirement is a small table, with size $O(max\_word\_length)$.

While BASE26s is unlikely to achieve great emulation fidelity it is lightweight and fast, and is expected to achieve a more realistic vocabulary than BASE26s.

Recurrent neural network   A better approach is to use observations from some real corpus to guide the construction of synthetic words. In the future we propose to train a character-level language model using a LSTM recurrent neural network (RNN) [49, 83]. The model would be trained on the lexicon file of an existing corpus, predicting one character at a time including an end-of-word character, therefore word length would be determined entirely by the RNN.

This method also requires a large lookup table (of size $O(|V|)$), to record words which have already been generated.

Markov models   Please note that the Markov word string generators discussed in this chapter are completely distinct from the Markov text generators referenced as WBMARKOV0, WB-MARKOV1, and STRINGMARKOVGEN, and introduced in Section 1.5.3. The Markov word-string generators are trained on letters within words, while the word-based Markov text generators are trained on the text of a corpus, with an "alphabet" consisting of words rather than letters.

Inspired by Shannon [79], our final method generates words from order-k Markov chains.[3] From a sample corpus we learn transition probabilities from every length-k prefix to every letter in our alphabet: for example, for $k = 2$ we learn, for each possible letter pair, the probability of each possible following letter. We represent the start of a word by k EOW (end of word) symbols. We can potentially achieve the word-length distribution we want by truncating the letter generation process for each word at a length sampled from the distribution.

Given a rank R_i, we draw a length L_i from a word-length model e.g., a left-truncated Gaussian; then, starting with k EOW symbols, we randomly walk the Markov chain to generate exactly L_i letters. If the resulting word was already generated for some other R_i, we try again up to a maximum of $|A|^{L_i}$ times. If that fails, we increment L_i and repeat the process.

We will see how well this form of length modeling works, in Section 6.5.4.

A downside of truncating at a fixed length is that the generated words look quite different from natural text, due to their endings. We can overcome this by introducing an EOW symbol and recording probabilities of transition to EOW. This makes more plausible words. CORPUS-GENERATOR implements both truncation to a length distribution and the version with an EOW symbol.

There are inevitably many zeroes in the transition matrix. This means that many letter sequences can never be generated. To address this, a smoothing method can be used. Rather than adding a small constant ϵ to all entries in the transision matrix and re-normalizing, smoothing is implemented by, with probability λ, falling back either to a lower-order transition matrix, or directly to the order-0 probabilities. For example, when looking for the next letter after "matri"

---

[3]See [38] for a modern text on Markov chains.

(order 5), smoothing might fall back to looking for a successor to "atri" (order 4) or even just pick a letter according to overall letter probabilities (order 0).

Smoothing increases the range of words which can be generated. It may also speed up processing, by reducing the probability that a candidate word has already been generated.

An important training question is whether the Markov model is trained using frequencies derived from distinct words in the vocabulary, or from word occurrences in the corpus. We expect that the latter will produce more realistic results and we use that method in our experiments.

If individual words such as the name of a chemical or the name of a potential takeover company reveal information, then it's possible that the high order Markov models may generate such trigger words and leak information about the training corpus. That could be mitigated by training the vocabulary on a similar corpus rather than the real one, but the degree of fidelity of emulation would also be reduced.

The CORPUSGENERATOR implementation uses a straightforward matrix representation with probabilities represented in double precision. With an alphabet size of 26, the maximum memory required is less than 3 GB for up to order 5. Going much beyond 5 is impractical with this implementation because the storage size increases by a factor of the alphabet size for each increment. Memory requirements could easily be reduced using sparse representations,[4] storing probabilities with less precision, or using a smaller alphabet. Sparse representations would almost certainly be required when generating a multi-lingual corpus, since the alphabet size would be far larger.

6.4.1   WORD STRING METHODS IN CORPUSGENERATOR

CORPUSGENERATOR implements:

Tnum – As described above. The letter "t" followed by the decimal representation of the word rank R_i.

Base26s – As described above. R_i expressed in base 26 using lowercase letters as the base 26 digits.

Base26s – As described above. A variant of BASE26 which achieves a much better distribution of word lengths.

SimpleWords – A heuristic method intended to achieve better word strings than TNUM while retaining the properties of speed and cache-friendliness. Readers are referred to the source code of SYNTHACORPUS for the precise details of this not very successful method.

Markov-? – As described above, the version of Markov without an EOW symbol. The "?" stands for the digit specifying the order of the model. Trained on word occurrences in the corpus.

Markov-?e – A version with an EOW symbol. Trained on word occurrences in the corpus.

---

[4]Such as the hash table method used in the WBMARKOV1 text generator. See Section 1.5.3.

Table 6.3: Illustrative examples of word strings generated by the various CORPUSGENERATOR methods at six different ranks in the word frequency ordering for emulations of the TREC-AP corpus. Markov word strings are dependent on the random seed. TNUM values are not as might be expected because words with equal frequency appear in arbitrary order.

Method	1	10	100	1,000	10,000	100,000
TNUM	t0	t9	t99	t999	t7999	t21289
BASE26	a	j	vd	lmb	puo	fnfg
BASE26S	a	j	kd	vob	fcoc	hnlesq
SIMPLEWORDS	bzb	kzkyk	ezeeye	qzqrbyq	qzqiryq	fzfahhyf
MARKOV-0	fda	cnwat	oeteyo	dhaaoptro	ssrbdaedeoo	efsfesryena
MARKOV-0E	ri	pl	eteraspdn	issc	sbvl	ecc
MARKOV-5	si	his	uphel	forcedings	statesmanl	curtisse
MARKOV-5E	the	have	pollone	use	struggle	dapena

Illustrative example word strings are given in Table 6.3.

CORPUSGENERATOR provides many additional options to control the behavior of the Markov word string generator. Unless otherwise specified, in the experiments reported in the following sections, we set $\lambda = 0$ (no smoothing). We trained on corpus rather than vocabulary frequencies.

The Markov word string generator provides optionally activated heuristics to try to achieve the desired correlation between word length and word frequency. The heuristic algorithm generates the required number of distinct words in an array and sorts the array by length. Then, in order of increasing length it randomly chooses a rank bucket, with probabilities determined by the rank distribution for words of this length. The word goes into the next free rank within the [logarithmic] rank bucket or spills into the next bucket if that bucket is already full.

The Markov word string generator also includes heuristics to estimate pronounceability of strings and to treat less pronounceable words as though they were longer when assigning word strings to word ranks.

Unless otherwise specified, both of these features were enabled during our experiments. Note that these heuristics could also be applied to methods such as BASE26S but would reduce the latter's speed advantage.

Text generators like the neural and Markov word- and string-based models, and encryption, don't explicitly create a vocabulary of word representations but produce a corpus from which the vocabulary may be extracted. Encryption may make substantial changes to the word strings in the vocabulary of the corpus. CAESAR1 preserves the original word lengths, and also the relationship between word lengths and frequency of occurrence. However, it changes the raw letter occurrence frequencies, but not the ranked letter occurrence frequencies. NOMENCLATOR potentially changes everything, depending upon the vocabulary mapping table.

6.5   EMPIRICAL STUDY OF METHODS

6.5.1   QUALITY OF WORD STRINGS

For most experimental purposes, we want synthetic words to "look like" real words. To evaluate our methods we compare $\mathbb{M}$ with $\mathbb{B}$ on a number of dimensions which are affected by the strings used to represent words.

1. Distribution of letters.

2. Distribution of letter bigrams.

3. Distribution of word lengths.

4. Correlation between word length and frequency of occurrence.

5. Compressibility of the resulting text.

6. Collision rates when inserting into a hash table.

We also assess the runtime and memory requirements taken by different methods to generate the lexicon for a corpus.

6.5.2   LETTER PROBABILITY DISTRIBUTIONS

Figures 6.5 and 6.6 show how well (or otherwise) the various word string generators are able to emulate the ranked letter probability distribution of a base corpus. CAEASAR1 does a perfect job, even though the relationship between letters and letter ranks has changed. In this case NOMENCLATOR achieves reasonable results but one cannot draw a general conclusion since the performance is totally dependent on the mapping table used. None of the other simple methods perform well. In the second figure, the Markov methods are shown to do a very good job of emulating the base on this dimension.

Figure 6.7 shows that the Markov methods continue to perform well on other corpora while BASE26s continues to perform poorly.

6.5.3   LETTER PAIR DISTRIBUTIONS

Figures 6.8 and 6.9 show that CAESAR1 and NOMENCLATOR with the particular mapping table do a good job of emulating the letter pair probability distribution. None of the other simple methods perform well, though SIMPLEWORDS does better than BASE26 and BASE26s. In the second figure, the Markov methods are shown to do a very good job of emulating the base on this dimension.

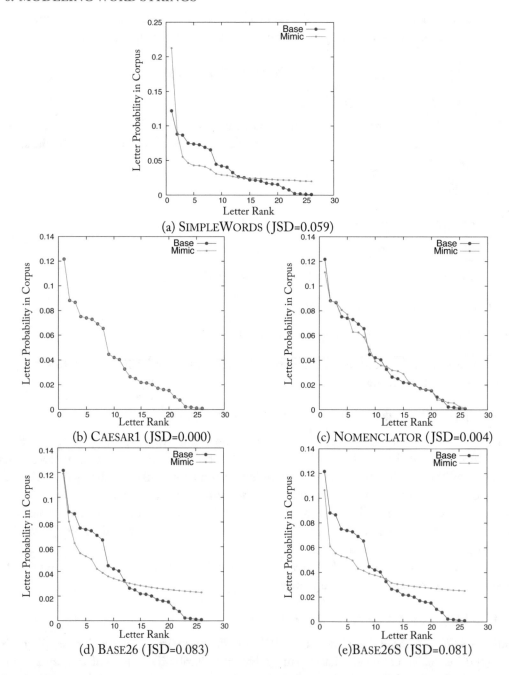

Figure 6.5: Comparing the letter probability distributions resulting from five different word string generators with the corresponding base distribution for the TREC-AP corpus.

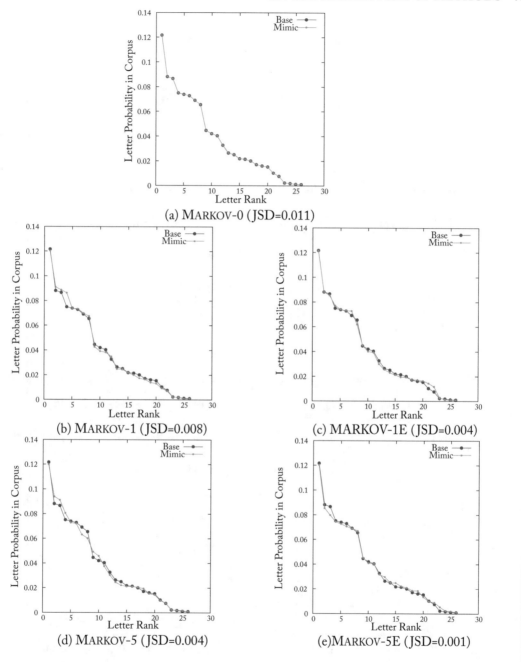

Figure 6.6: Comparing the letter probability distributions resulting from five different Markov word string generators with the corresponding base distribution for the TREC-AP corpus. One trial per condition.

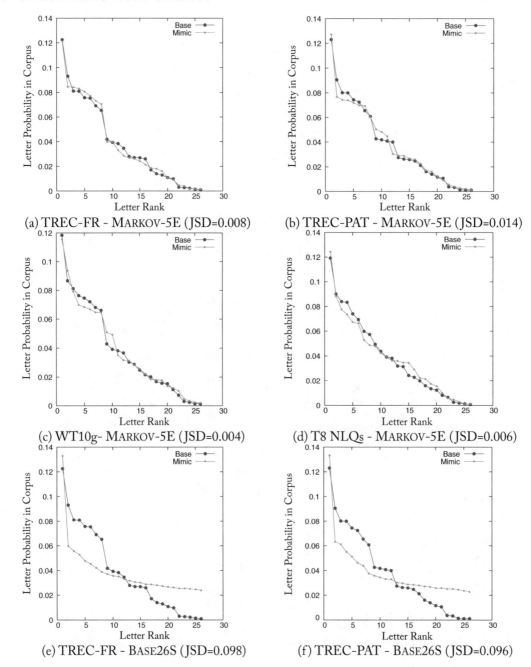

Figure 6.7: Markov-5e modeling of letter probability distributions for a selection of other corpora. The bottom row shows Base26s modeling of two of the corpora for comparison.

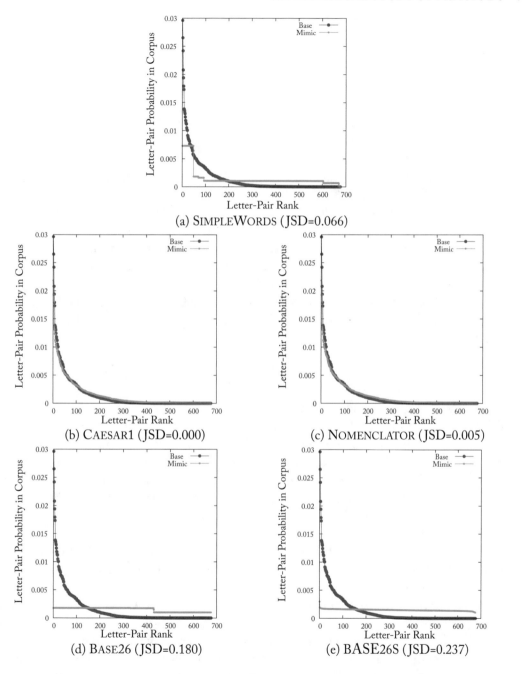

(a) SIMPLEWORDS (JSD=0.066)

(b) CAESAR1 (JSD=0.000)

(c) NOMENCLATOR (JSD=0.005)

(d) BASE26 (JSD=0.180)

(e) BASE26S (JSD=0.237)

Figure 6.8: Comparing the letter pair probability distributions resulting from five different word string generators with the corresponding base distribution for the TREC-AP corpus.

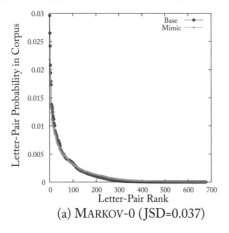

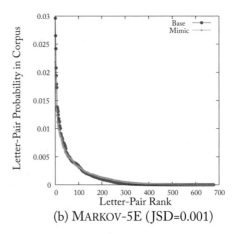

(a) MARKOV-0 (JSD=0.037)   (b) MARKOV-5E (JSD=0.001)

Figure 6.9: Comparing the letter pair probability distributions resulting from different Markov word string generators with the corresponding base distribution for the TREC-AP corpus. One trial per condition. The plots for MARKOV-1, MARKOV-1E, and MARKOV-5 are nearly identical to that of MARKOV-5E with JSD values ranging from 0.002–0.004. Corresponding plots for MARKOV-5E on TREC-FR, TREC-AP, WT10g, and T8 NLQs are very similar, with JSD = 0.002 in each case.

6.5.4   WORD LENGTH DISTRIBUTIONS

Figure 6.10 shows the distribution of word lengths for the vocabulary of the TREC-AP corpus and for various emulated vocabularies. As can be seen, the base distribution is a nice bell-shaped curve and, of course, CAESAR1 matches it exactly. NOMENCLATOR also matches it exactly, but the degree of match is completely dependent upon the NOMENCLATOR table. In the experiments reported in this chapter, the right-hand side of the NOMENCLATOR table was just a randomized version of the left hand side. BASE26S also achieves a very high degree of match, but the other low-cost word generation methods TNUM (not shown), BASE26 and SIMPLEWORDS do a very poor job of matching the distribution.

Figure 6.11 compares variants of Markov word string generation. Each of them achieves reasonably good emulation of the word length distribution. The variants relying on an EOW symbol perform somewhat worse than those which don't.

Consider first the case of the variants which don't use an EOW symbol. The lengths are modeled as a normal distribution whose mean and standard deviation are calculated from the actual distribution, but modified using heuristic correction factors to try to compensate for the left truncation of the distribution at length one. A further distorting factor is that the number of possible very short words is limited. There are only 26 possible words of length one. If the Markov string generator chooses one which has already been generated, the generation process will be restarted.

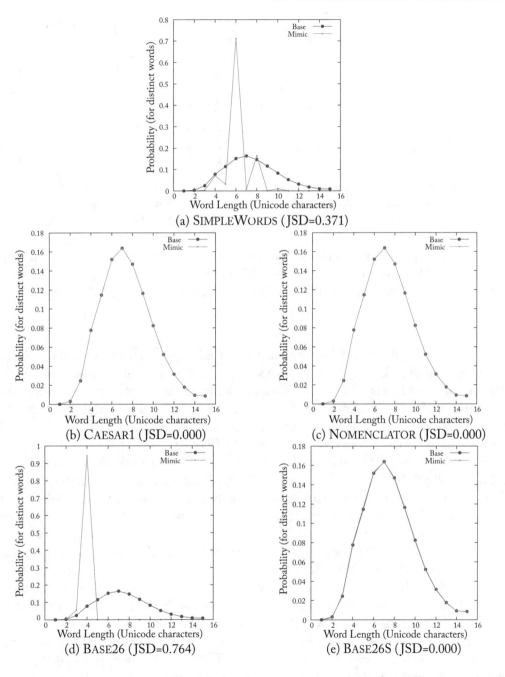

(a) SIMPLEWORDS (JSD=0.371)

(b) CAESAR1 (JSD=0.000)

(c) NOMENCLATOR (JSD=0.000)

(d) BASE26 (JSD=0.764)

(e) BASE26S (JSD=0.000)

Figure 6.10: Comparing the word length distributions resulting from five different word string generators with the corresponding base distribution for the TREC-AP corpus.

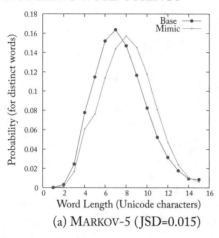

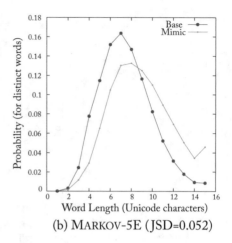

(a) MARKOV-5 (JSD=0.015)   (b) MARKOV-5E (JSD=0.052)

Figure 6.11: Comparing the word length distributions resulting from Markov word string generators, with and without EOW modeling, with the corresponding base distribution for the TREC-AP corpus. One trial per condition. Plots for Markov orders 0 and 1 show similar shapes.

Next, consider the case of MARKOV-0E, where the length is determined by the probability of occurrence of the EOW symbol. If there were no limit on how many distinct words there were of a particular length, then we would expect the word lengths to form a geometric distribution, with highest probability at length 1 and a monotonic decrease in probability after that. The absolute limit on the number of distinct words of very short lengths radically alters this distribution, but the effect is even stronger due to the fact that some sequences of letters are very unlikely. For example, the probability that the next sequence generated from a model trained on TREC-AP will be "qqq" is of the order of 10^{-13}. For the corpus frequencies emulation of TREC-AP by MARKOV-0E, shown in Figure 6.13, only about 55% of the possible 3-letter words were generated. The kick-up at length 15 is due to the fact that a maximum of 15 characters is imposed on the length of words.

Figure 6.13 shows that the kick-up is exaggerated when the frequencies used in training the MARKOV-0E model on TREC-AP are taken from the vocabulary list rather than the corpus. In that case the probability of seeing an EOW symbol is reduced from 0.1708 to 0.1169.

Unfortunately, observations on some other corpora paint a less desirable picture. In Figure 6.12, T8 NLQs shows a similar bell-like curve to TREC-AP and MARKOV-5E emulates it well. However, the other three corpora show quite irregular patterns and the MARKOV-5E method emulates them poorly. For TREC-FR and TREC-PAT where MARKOV-5E performs poorly, BASE26s performs very well.

Figure 6.14 attempts to show how well the simple word string generators capture the relationship between word length and word frequency of occurrence. Each point represents the

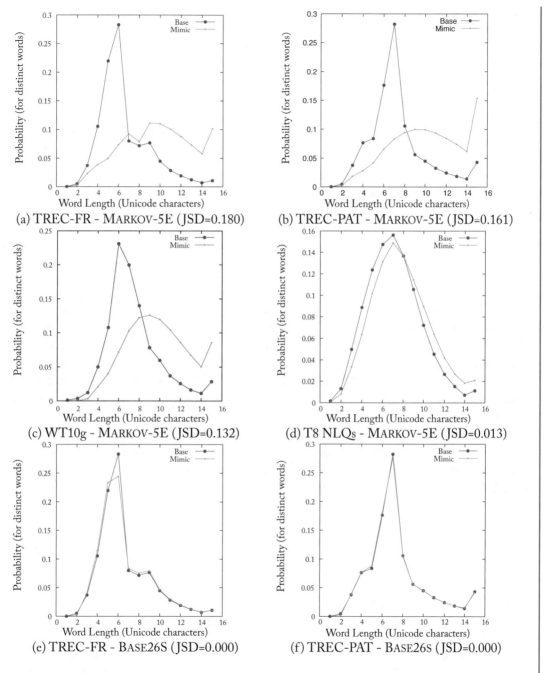

Figure 6.12: MARKOV-5E modeling of word length distributions for a selection of other corpora. The bottom row shows BASE26S modeling of two of the corpora for comparison.

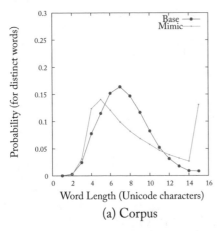
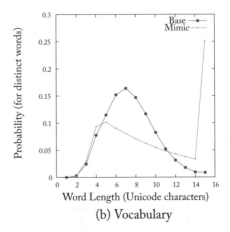

(a) Corpus   (b) Vocabulary

Figure 6.13: TREC-AP: The word length distribution for the MARKOV-0E method using probabilities derived from (a) the corpus and (b) the vocabulary.

average occurrence frequency for words of a given length against that length. Unsurprisingly, CAESAR1 achieves a perfect match, but all the other methods show a very poor match. Although BASE26s models the distribution of word lengths very well, it does not capture the relationship between word length and frequency of occurrence. NOMENCLATOR performs quite poorly because although the words on the right hand side of the NOMENCLATOR table match the real distribution of word lengths, the relationship between word length and occurrence frequency is broken.

Our runs with the EOW version of the Markov generator activated the heuristic to try to achieve a realistic correlation between word length and frequency of occurrence. Figure 6.15 shows how well this works over a range of corpora. Despite the irregularities in the base plots, the MARKOV-5E matching is reasonably good.

6.5.5   COMPRESSIBILITY OF TEXT

Table 6.4 shows how the compressibility of $\mathbb{M}$ varies from that of $\mathbb{B}$ according to which word string generator is used. As expected, the CAESAR1 method leaves compressibility unchanged. All of the Markov methods (the corpus generators WBMARKOV0, WBMARKOV1, and STRING-MARKOVGEN, and the word string generators), simpleWords, and both BASE26 variants tend to reduce the compressibility of the corpus while NOMENCLATOR (with the mapping table used) increases it.

Compressibility needs to be considered in the context of the size of the corpus, as some word string generators inflate the size of the text and may increase the redundancy. Table 6.5 shows that the only method (NOMENCLATOR) which increased compressibility also significantly inflated the size of the corpus. Even though the words in the vocabulary are exactly the same,

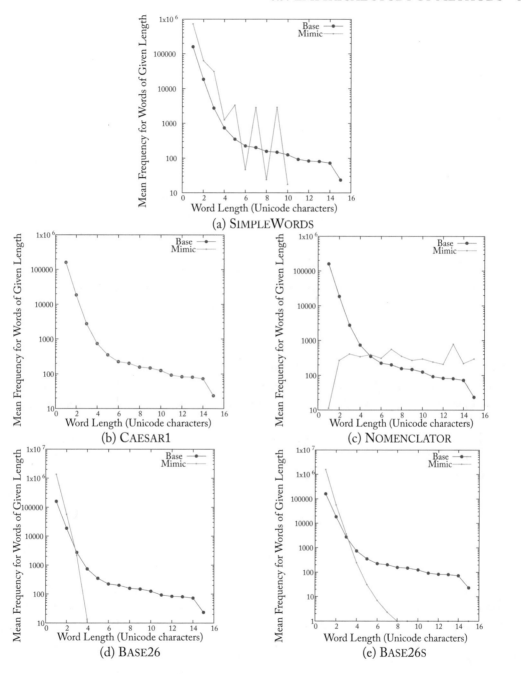

Figure 6.14: Relation between word length and word frequency for the TREC-AP corpus and a range of simple word string generation methods.

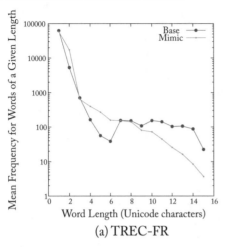

(a) TREC-FR

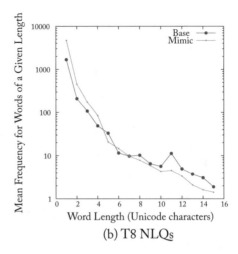

(b) T8 NLQs

Figure 6.15: Relation between word length and word frequency for two corpora and the MARKOV-5E word string generator. One trial per condition. Modeling accuracy in plots for TREC-AP, TREC-PAT, TREC-all, and WT10g generally falls between those of these two plots.

NOMENCLATOR increases the text size by disrupting the correlation between word length and word frequency. Although the ratios shown for the two STRINGMARKOVGEN methods appear identical, there are very small differences in sizes between the generated corpora. (i.e., it's not a mistake!)

For every corpus, each higher-order Markov method shows a closer compressibility score to the original than the lower-order version: WBMARKOV1 v. WBMARKOV0; STRINGMARKOV-GEN/13 v. STRINGMARKOVGEN/5; and MARKOV-5E v. MARKOV-1E.

6.5.6 RESOURCE REQUIREMENTS AND VOCABULARY STRUCTURE PERFORMANCE

As previously noted, the CPU and memory requirements of a word string generator are important considerations.

We must also consider the way generated words behave in typical components of an IR system. A wide range of vocabulary accumulation structures are reviewed by Heinz et al. [47]. Comparing the suitability of synthetically generated words against all of these methods is beyond the scope of the present work, but as a sanity check, we consider the rate of hash collisions—that is, how many words share hashes? This clearly depends crucially on the choice of hash function and table size, but serves to illustrate the sorts of downstream processing needed in a real IR system. The goal is not, of course, to minimize collisions; rather it is to generate words which behave similarly to those in the seed corpus.

Table 6.4: Relative compressibility of text generated using different word string generators while holding other simulation parameters constant. Compressibility is the ratio of uncompressed to compressed size after using gzip with default settings. Shown here is the ratio of the compressibility of $\mathbb{M}$ relative to that of $\mathbb{B}$. Note that WBMarkov0, WBMarkov1, and string-MarkovGen are corpus generators which incidentally produce a vocabulary, while Markov-1e and Markov-5e are word string generators.

	TREC -AP	TREC -FR	TREC -PAT	TREC -all	WT10g	T8 NLQs
Caesar1	1.000	1.000	1.000	1.000	1.000	1.000
Nomenclator	1.176	1.100	1.143	1.223	1.123	1.132
WBMarkov0	0.901	0.669	0.598	0.816	0.716	0.713
WBMarkov1	0.935	0.709	0.634	0.838	0.747	0.769
StringMark. $k = 5$	0.942	9.725	0.659	0.849	0.778	0.832
StringMark. $k = 13$	0.955	0.752	0.680	0.861	0.797	0.841
Base26	0.707	0.495	0.450	0.643	0.591	0.812
Base26s	0.699	0.497	0.448	0.648	0.600	0.772
SimpleWords	0.954	0.674	0.621	0.862	0.785	0.812
Markov-1e	0.852	0.638	0.572	0.765	0.696	0.736
Markov-5e	0.906	0.696	0.617	0.829	0.739	0.733

Table 6.6 compares the corpusGenerator word string generators on several resource and performance dimensions:

- Hashing collision statistics relative to the base vocabulary—Total number of collisions and maximum collision chain length, each expressed as a percentage of the value for the base. Each word, in order, from an alphabetically sorted vocabulary list was inserted into the hash table once.

- Memory requirements of the word string generator in megabytes. The values for the Markov methods are represented as the sum of the sizes of the (dense) transition matrices and the hash table needed to prevent emission of duplicate word strings.

- Time taken per word generated. This is represented as both the mean time per word in microseconds, and as the mean number of tries needed to ensure a unique word. Times should be regarded as indicative only, as we only performed one run.

All experiments used the WT10g corpus and were run on NewMac (see Section 1.8.2). The vocabulary size was approximately 5.4 million words. We used a power of two hashtable of

Table 6.5: Size ratio of text generated using different word string generators while holding other simulation parameters constant. Note that size includes minimal markup, i.e., DOC, DOCNO, and TEXT elements.

	TREC -AP	TREC -FR	TREC -PAT	TREC -all	WT10g	T8 NLQs
CAESAR1	1.000	1.000	1.000	1.000	1.000	1.000
NOMENCLATOR	1.435	1.223	1.392	1.552	1.404	1.254
WBMARKOV0	0.997	0.978	0.999	0.978	0.997	0.937
WBMARKOV1	0.999	0.981	1.002	1.003	1.033	0.868
STRINGMARK. k=5	0.977	0.921	0.944	0.946	0.917	0.832
STRINGMARK. k=13	0.977	0.921	0.944	0.946	0.917	0.832
BASE26	0.541	0.500	0.521	0.537	0.583	0.783
BASE26S	0.537	0.488	0.515	0.523	0.573	0.797
SIMPLEWORDS	0.926	0.865	0.917	0.911	0.976	0.935
MARKOV-1E	0.979	1.001	1.007	0.961	1.019	0.936
MARKOV-5E	0.995	1.017	1.030	0.993	1.025	0.948

size 2^{23} (approximately 8.4 million entries). No bucketing was used. If a collision occurred, a new location was found by relatively prime rehashing, taking advantage of the fact that any odd hash step is relatively prime with a power of two table size. We used the FNV-1a [66] hashing function.

Results and Discussion

The average number of collisions per insertion for the base vocabulary was approximately **0.7** and the maximum number of collisions for any insertion was **39**.

The choice of word string method has almost no effect on hash collision rate. Although the variations in maximum collision chain length are larger, they are still quite small for what is expected to be a quite volatile measure.

The TNUM, BASE26, and SIMPLEWORDS methods are very fast—they generate of the order of 10^8 word strings per second. The BASE26S method is three orders of magnitude slower than BASE26. It does require floating point calculations and a table, but we believe that the main reason for the difference is that the time from which the mean times are calculated includes the time to build the sparsity table from the base vocabulary.

The results for the Markov word string methods show that 160 MB of memory is required for the hash table used to avoid duplicates, regardless of the order k of the model. Because the

Table 6.6: WT10g: Summary characteristics of the word string generation methods relating to hash table collisions, and resources required to generate the vocabulary. Percentages are relative to the corresponding value for $\mathbb{B}$.

	Hash		State	Per Word	
	Collisions	Max Chain	Memory (MB)	μs	Tries
TNUM	97.1%	84.6%	0	0.013	1.000
BASE26	108.2%	102.6%	0	0.010	1.000
BASE26S	97.7%	94.9%	Tiny table	10.275	1.000
SIMPLEWORDS	100.2%	82.1%	0	0.019	1.000
MARKOV-0	101.6%	84.6%	0.000 + 160.000	18.365	104.843
MARKOV-0E	100.3%	107.7%	0.000 + 160.000	0.904	2.115
MARKOV-1	100.8%	76.9%	0.006 + 160.000	42.982	328.064
MARKOV-1E	100.3%	87.2%	0.006 + 160.000	1.163	3.128
MARKOV-5	100.6%	84.6%	2955.784 + 160.000	944.170	2149.049
MARKOV-5E	100.4%	97.4%	3069.468 + 160.000	36.114	104.138

transition matrices are stored densely, the memory they require is negligible for small values of k and very large—proportional to 27^k—for large values.

The times reported for the Markov word string methods also include the time taken to learn the transition matrices. The table shows a huge difference in generation times between the Markov methods with an EOW symbol and those without. The versions without EOW are at least a factor of 20 slower, and require at least 20 times as many tries to come up with a word which hasn't been generated before. This seems odd because the heuristics for achieving better correlation between word length and word frequency are only applied to the EOW versions. They should add to the time taken. At this stage we do not have an explanation.

We note that the BASE26 and BASE26S methods do not rely on shared read-write structures and could easily be multi-threaded. However, methods (all the others) which can potentially generate the same word at different ranks would require locking of the hashtable used to detect and avoid this.

We also note that the results in Table 6.6 are only indicative. To gain an accurate picture of the relative merits of different word string generators with respect to accuracy of emulation of the base corpus vocabulary in its interaction with vocabulary lookup structures, we would need to repeat the observations for several different lookup structures and for several different corpora. We would need to similarly expand the scope of the experiment in order to properly compare the speed of the methods.

6.6   WORD STRINGS FROM GPT-2 AND MARKOV METHODS

The GPT-2 generator doesn't start out by explicitly generating representational strings for each word in the vocabulary. However, in the course of generating text, it inevitably creates a set of distinct word strings which make up the vocabulary. Many of those word strings match those in the base corpus, however it does create a lot which were not. Figure 6.17 gives an example fragment of GPT-2-generated text which includes the words scoularator, toefine, beelzebufe, and duckisition which are not present in the base corpus.

The same figure also illustrates the text generated by the word-based order-one WB-Markov1 method, which is constrained to use only words from the base vocabulary, and the stringMarkovGen method with $k = 23$, $\lambda = 0$.

As shown in Figure 6.16, GPT-2 does a good job of emulating the distribution of TREC-AP word lengths and a reasonable job of modeling the correlation between word length and word frequency of occurrence. WBMarkov1 and stringMarkovGen with $k = 23$, $\lambda = 0$ also perform well. Please note that each of the three generators is a random process and that the plots in the figures represent just one possible output from each.

All three are likely to leak a lot of information from the base corpus. For example, a web search reveals some real people with the name Robbie Riedel, although none seemed to be "stenographer actor turned models."

6.7   DISCUSSION

The word lists produced by the higher-order Markov methods we implemented show quite good distributions of length, unigram frequency, and bigram frequency. Particularly with smoothing enabled, they are capable of generating vocabularies far larger than the one used for training. Subjectively, there is a plausibility to many of the words they generate, e.g., "bayesiant," "biopestive," and "relaxationalco." Using an EOW symbol rather than cutting off at a pre-determined length results in more natural word endings but at a cost of less accurate modeling of word lengths. For a reason not yet properly understood, the EOW version runs much faster than the plain version. The heuristics we employed to achieve better correlation between word length and word frequency seem to work reasonably well.

A point to consider when deciding between a Markov method with an EOW symbol and one without, is that many IR systems rely on stemming and word-breaking. It's unclear that such lexical operations can be well supported by either variant of the current Markov word generator but words comprising arbitrarily truncated strings seem likely to be much inferior. In future work, one could consider training a Markov model whose alphabet consisted of morphemes rather than letters, to better model this dimension.

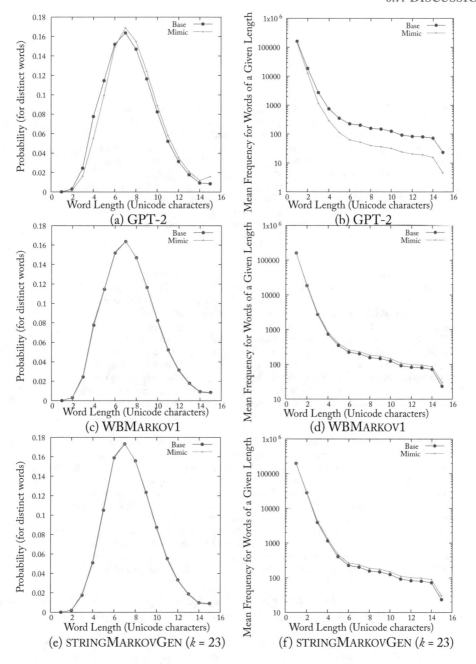

Figure 6.16: Comparison of the characteristics of the word strings generated by GPT-2 and Markov emulations of the TREC-AP corpus. Left is the distribution of word lengths. Right is the relationship between word length and word frequency.

stenographer actor turned model robbie riedel is sweeping america
whose first love was proximity and know how for the first time he has
made an art form his own sex sex itself a sexy look stateside magazine
said vogue magazine said in its june 12 issue debussy was lucky to be
alive at all another few seconds from closes for donaldson s ashes as
his scythe clutches its targets the hulking scoularator the apple
tournament larry the most outspoken judge in the u s toefine the chain
what will become effective is no doubt beelzebufe of north redfern
affirmative comment let s face it geoffrey donaldson geefinity but
lachlan probably best news there is all he does is take notes on the
proceedings on the row over the bogus duckisition ....

a taiwanese authorities said hospital s office you think it s criminal
counts of all really go marching today that is his life for last seen
in beirut according to wear light on to the rockaway facility u s
whereabouts philip morris said 30 a laughter and they conspired to
respond the utility vehicle the other assault charge cannons and the
offensive manner carrying the average of 1989 peace then smelled
liquor store other major stories but according the photos annotated
reprint of the total memory two other factions including casting of
the higher the times a share warner bros 3 3 000 maintenence worker
unrest neither you will welcome but they really wanda moore the rebel
proposal would delete reference to smooth to prevent rather than it s

civil defense warning sirens a thing of the past communities say the civil
defense siren that cold war symbol of the fear of a soviet nuclear attack
that doctrine known as mad for mutually assured destruction is based on the
theory that mobil expects billion from the sale of property in new jersey
and england the results included a non recurring net gain of million or
cents a share compared with million or per share for the fiscal quarter
ended may of a share up from cents in the comparable period a year earlier
cars and trucks made in the united states according to a new radio channel
the government set up state corporations staffed largely by officials fearful
of making even trivial decisions and by the will of the palestinian people
he said the organization s member house of delegates a legislative body

Figure 6.17: **Examples of emulated text generated by GPT-2 (top) and WBMarkov1 (center) and stringMarkovGen (k = 23, bottom) methods based on the TREC-AP corpus.**

The tendency of the Markov process to repeatedly generate the same strings substantially increases its memory and CPU requirements, due to the need for a lookup structure to detect and reject the repetitions.

Because BASE26s cannot generate repeated strings, it requires only a small table of skip values (15 in our case), and operates much faster than the Markov methods. Single threaded on our hardware, it is capable of generating almost 5 million words per second. Speed of generation can easily be improved by multi-threading and probably by code optimization.

However, generating a scaled-up vocabulary using BASE26s would require a model of how the skip table entries change with vocabulary size. That remains for future work.

A disadvantage of the BASE26s method is that words sorted by rank are also sorted by length, i.e., all the n-letter words have lower ranks than any of the words with $n + 1$ letters. A solution to this might lie in using the length model to choose the length L of a word and then using the skip value for L to compute a word number. An extra counter for each length and a fallback mechanism would be needed to ensure that repeated words were not generated but total memory requirement would still be only around 30 numbers.

Reproducibility of experiments involving synthetic word generation is an important desideratum. BASE26 for an agreed alphabet is inherently reproducible and BASE26s requires only the additional sharing of a small table of skip values. Reproducible word generation by the stochastic methods is more challenging. It requires communication of the random seed, and the table of parameters to the length model. A reproducible Markov generator would additionally require communication of the transition matrix.

CHAPTER 7

Models of Corpus Growth

Both in industry and in research, it is desirable that the runtime of IR algorithms should grow no faster than linearly with the size of the problem. An algorithm is said to be *scalable* if its running time increases linearly with size.

For some important IR algorithms the size of the problem is measured by the size of the corpus, but we must be careful how we measure size. As noted in Section 1.7.1, size in bytes is not appropriate because corpora differ in characteristics that may affect IR algorithms, and are inflated to different degrees by mark-up, whitespace, and character representations. Scalability experimentation needs a series of corpora of different sizes, with homogeneous properties and homogeneous representation.

The aim of work reported in this chapter is to provide a valid basis on which studies of algorithm scalability can make use of synthetic corpora many times larger than a base corpus. In other words, we would like to extract the model parameter values from a base corpus and use a growth model to predict what the values of those parameters would be if the corpus were scaled up by a factor of k.

Note that all the properties discussed in previous chapters on corpus emulation are important in scaling up. We want experiments conducted on $\mathbb{S}$, a scaled-up version of $\mathbb{B}$, to accurately predict observations obtained in the future when $\mathbb{B}$ grows to the size of $\mathbb{S}$.

In the absence of a better alternative, we assume that the base corpus is an unbiased sample of an infinite parent corpus. Scaling up the base corpus by a factor of k can be seen as drawing a sample k times as large from the parent. This model provides a sound basis for studies of the scalability of IR algorithms.

Of the text generation methods discussed in Chapter 1 some are more suitable than others for emulating corpus growth. The encryption methods are clearly unsuitable. Topic modeling is unlikely to be suitable in the absence of scalable topic models and generators. Simple language models such as BASELINE, WBMARKOV0, and WBMARKOV1 face the problem of constrained vocabularies. Neural and string-based Markov models seem better placed in that regard. Finally, macro-properties generators can create scaled-up corpora when coupled with a model of corpus growth.

We discuss macro-properties generators first, then Markov and neural generators.

Table 7.1: Corpus growth model. The parameters are the same as for the static model with $s = 1, h = 10$ but here we show how they vary as the corpus sample size increases. G is the factor by which the sample size is increased.

Sample Size	1%	2%	5%	10%	20%	50%	100%
Number of Samples	7	6	5	4	3	2	1

7.1   SCALING UP OF MACRO PROPERTIES

We derived growth models by randomly sampling documents from each base corpus to create samples ranging from 1–100% of the original. We drew multiple samples of each size and took the average of the parameter values for each size. To heuristically correct for greater variability in small samples, the smaller the sample size, the more samples we averaged. We then plotted the change in value of each parameter for each base corpus against sample size and determined, by inspection, the nature of the relationship. These relationships are summarized in Table 7.1.

Figures 7.1–7.4 show the change in the various property values with increasing sample size.

We excluded the TREC-PAT corpus from our sampling and scaling experiments as it comprises less than 7000 documents. In its place we used the TREC-WSJ corpus which has the advantage that, like TREC-AP, it is a time-ordered corpus.

Unsurprisingly, the mean and standard deviation of document length hardly change with change in sample size. The same is true for gamma shape and scale. The percentage of the vocabulary accounted for by words which occur only once can also be approximated as a constant. Figure 7.1 shows that the percentage decreases with scale-up in some corpora, increases in others, and remains steady in yet others.

The proportion of word occurrences accounted for by each of the ten highest frequency words is also approximately constant; see Figure 7.2.

When modeling the middle part of the ranked word frequency distribution according to Zipf's law, the exponent α increases roughly linearly with sample size, but with a quite small slope; see Figure 7.3. Obviously, the number of postings grows linearly with sample size.

As seen in Figure 7.4, vocabulary size grows in proportion to a fractional power of the scale-up factor. This growth is consistent with laws due to Herdan and Heaps. Interestingly, Baeza-Yates and Navarro [6] show that text generated from a finite state machine operating in the same fashion as Miller's monkey [63] will conform to both Zipf's and Heaps's laws and that the exponents of both laws are related.

Our growth model was developed assuming the use of the CORPUSGENERATOR parameters $h = 10, s = 1$. Growth modeling of S, the 4-tuples describing each piecewise segment is expected to be "fragile," and time has not permitted us to explore it. This remains for future work.

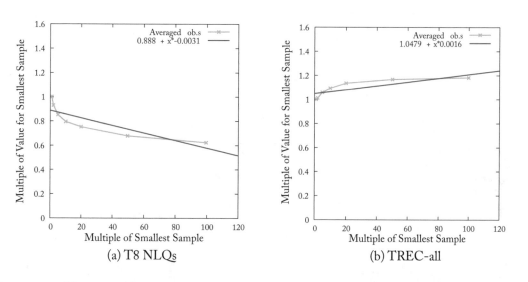

Figure 7.1: Change in the percentage of vocabulary singletons (w_1) with increasing scale-up factor. Linear axes. Plots for TREC-WSJ, TREC-AP, TREC-FR, and WT10g are similar but with lines of best fit closer to horizontal.

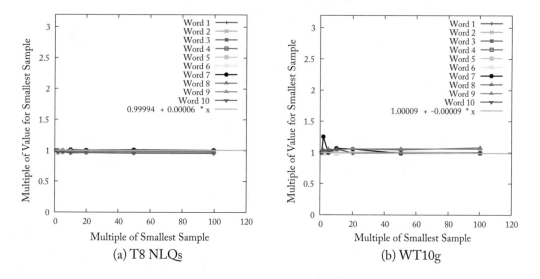

Figure 7.2: Change in the proportion of word occurrences accounted for by each of the 10 most popular words with increasing scale-up factor. Linear axes. Plots for TREC-WSJ, TREC-AP, TREC-FR, and TREC-all are similar.

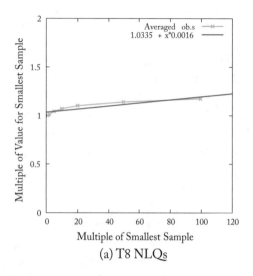 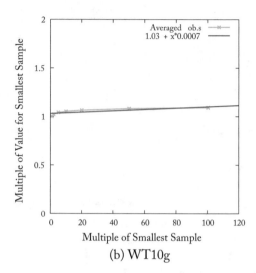

(a) T8 NLQs   (b) WT10g

Figure 7.3: Change in the magnitude of the Zipf α exponent for the middle section of the distribution with increasing scale-up factor. Linear axes. Plots for TREC-WSJ, TREC-AP, TREC-FR, and TREC-all are similar.

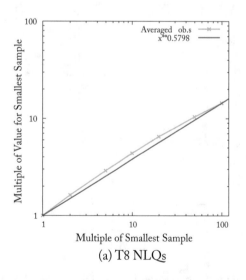 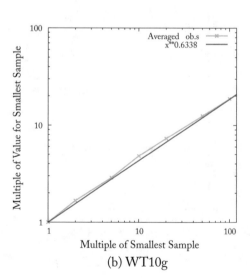

(a) T8 NLQs   (b) WT10g

Figure 7.4: Change in vocabulary size with increasing scale-up factor. Log log plots. Plots for TREC-WSJ, TREC-AP, TREC-FR, and TREC-all are similar.

When simulating the growth of a base corpus, it would be convenient to avoid the need to derive corpus-specific growth models for each new dataset. In the future we hope to explore the use of a generic model obtained by averaging over several corpora.

7.1.1   EFFECTS OF CORPUS GROWTH ON TERM DEPENDENCY

The discussion in the previous section and Figure 7.3 relate to growth modeling with an assumption of word independence. In this section we take a preliminary look at how word dependence changes with increase in corpus size, by examining the distribution of bigram frequencies.

Figure 7.5 suggests that the highest frequency of a 2-gram existing in a sample corpus grows linearly with sample size. For each of the corpora the slope is very close to 1.

The plots for the other 2-gram parameters (Figures 7.6 and 7.7) suggest power law relationships. The definition of "significant bigram" is given in Section 5.1. For 2-gram α the growth exponent is small. For five of the corpora it is positive, while T8 NLQs is the exception. It shows a small negative growth exponent.

7.1.2   SIMULATING TEMPORAL GROWTH

In news corpora such as TREC-AP and TREC-WSJ there is a natural temporal ordering of the documents. In these cases, the corpus grows as new events happen and journalists report them. It is natural to ask whether the "progressively larger samples from an infinite corpus" model applies to the natural growth of news corpora.

We studied this using the TREC news corpora by taking successively larger temporal subsets, observing changes in properties as we did with samples, and comparing temporal growth models with those developed in the preceding section. We focus our attention on vocabulary size and word frequency distribution.

Figure 7.8 shows the rate of growth in vocabulary size and Zipf α. Looking at the top pair of graphs we see that, in both cases, the rate of growth in vocabulary size is very slightly faster in the temporal case. This may imply that the vocabulary of the smallest temporal subsets is smaller than that of samples of equivalent sizes due to greater topic coherence in news items covering a narrow time period. However, the effect is negligible.

In Section 7.1.4 we report some comparisons between corpora scaled up from samples and those scaled up from temporal subsets.

7.1.3   FACILITIES IN SYNTHACORPUS

SYNTHACORPUS provides the following capabilities:

selectRecordsFromFile Performs either random sampling or temporal selection from the file representing a corpus. Temporal selection assumes that the corpus file is in date order and just takes the first N documents.

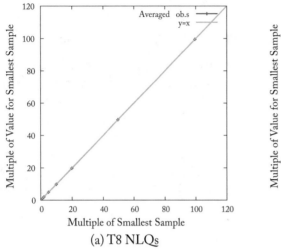 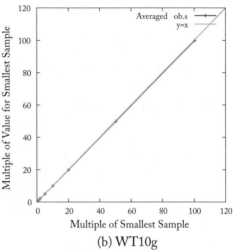

(a) T8 NLQs   (b) WT10g

Figure 7.5: Variation of highest 2-gram frequency with corpus size. Linear axes. Plots for TREC-WSJ, TREC-AP, TREC-FR, and TREC-all are similar.

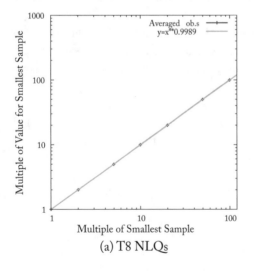 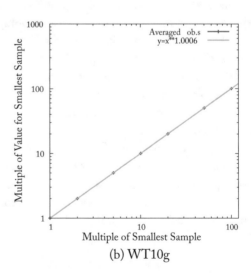

(a) T8 NLQs   (b) WT10g

Figure 7.6: Variation of number of significant 2-grams with corpus size. Log log plots. Plots for TREC-WSJ, TREC-AP, TREC-FR, and TREC-all are similar.

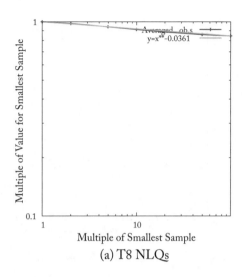

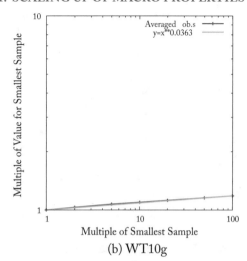

(a) T8 NLQs

(b) WT10g

Figure 7.7: Variation of 2-gram exponent α with corpus size. Log log plots. Plots for TREC-WSJ, TREC-AP, TREC-FR, and TREC-all are similar to that of WT10g.

Table 7.2: Details of sample sizes used in studying collection growth

Parameter	Growth Function	Additional Information
$H_1 \dots H_h$	Constant	
w_1	Treated as constant	
α	Linear	
P	Linear	
$|V|$	$|V| \times G^\beta$	$\beta < 1$
dl mean	Constant	
dl st. dev.	Constant	
dl gamma shape	Constant	
dl gamma scale	Constant	

samplingExperiments.pl Repeatedly uses SELECTRECORDSFROMFILE to make samples of the sizes from Table 7.2, extracts their properties and makes a growth model.

scaleUpASample.pl Uses the growth model generated by SAMPLINGEXPERIMENTS.PL to derive parameters for a scaled up corpus, then calls CORPUSGENERATOR to create such a corpus. If the resulting scaled up corpus has the same size as the original base corpus $\mathbb{B}$ it can compare the scaled-up sample $\mathbb{S}$ with $\mathbb{B}$.

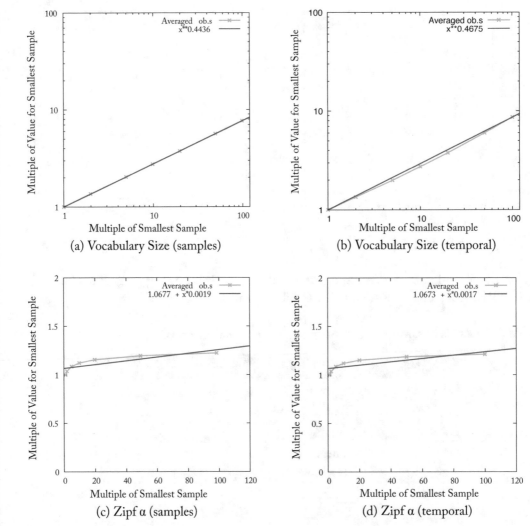

Figure 7.8: TREC-AP corpus: Comparison of growth in vocabulary size (top row, log log axes) and Zipf α (bottom row) for sampling (left-hand side) and temporal growth (right-hand side). Plots for the other temporal growth corpus TREC-WSJ are similar.

7.1.4   MACRO-PROPERTIES SCALE-UP EXPERIMENTS

We used the SAMPLINGEXPERIMENTS.PL script to derive growth models from the 1, 2, 5, 10, 20, 50, and 100% samples and temporal subsets. Note that there is only one growth model for sampling and one for temporal subsets. Everything in a growth model is expressed relative to the smallest sample or subset.

We then used scaleUpASample.pl to take corpusGenerator parameters for 1, 10, and 50% samples or subsets, and the relevant growth model to calculate the parameters needed to scale up the sample to 100%. We then ran corpusGenerator to create a corpus, and compared its properties with those of the original base corpus. If we have a perfect growth model, then the properties of the scaled-up corpus $\mathbb{S}$ should be as close to $\mathbb{B}$ as if we used corpusPropertyExtractor and corpusGenerator to emulate it directly.

We used gamma modeling of document lengths, $h = 10$, $s = 1$ for modeling the word frequency distribution, and Markov-5e as the word-string generator.

7.1.5   RESULTS OF MACRO-PROPERTIES SCALE-UP

Figures 7.9–7.10 present the results of attempting to emulate the properties of a base corpus by scaling up samples. A number of observations may be made:

1. There is no appreciable difference between the plots for samples and for temporal growth.

2. Figure 7.9 shows surprisingly little benefit from using larger samples.

3. The deficiency of using only one piecewise segment to model the middle section of the word frequency distribution is very apparent.

4. Singleton words are appropriately modeled but one needs to look very closely to see them because of the pronounced discontinuity of the linear segment and the singletons.

5. Modeling of the distribution of document lengths is very good, with small JSD.

6. Unsurprisingly, the bigram frequency distribution is very poorly modeled.

7. Modeling of the distribution of word lengths is very good, but the modeling of the relationship between word length and word frequency is erratic.

7.2   HOW WELL DO MARKOV METHODS MODEL GROWTH?

MarkovGenerator and stringMarkovGen can be told to generate a corpus of arbitrary size, i.e., they can generate a quantity of text larger than the quantity on which they were trained. These methods are described in Section 1.5.3.

Word-based Markov generators like MarkovGenerator suffer from the fundamental limitation that they are constrained to produce a vocabulary no larger than that of the corpus on which they were trained. Scaling up from a training sample results in a violation of the law due to Herdan and Heaps. Note that applying smoothing to the word-based Markov model allows for the generation of unseen sequences of words, but can't create new words.

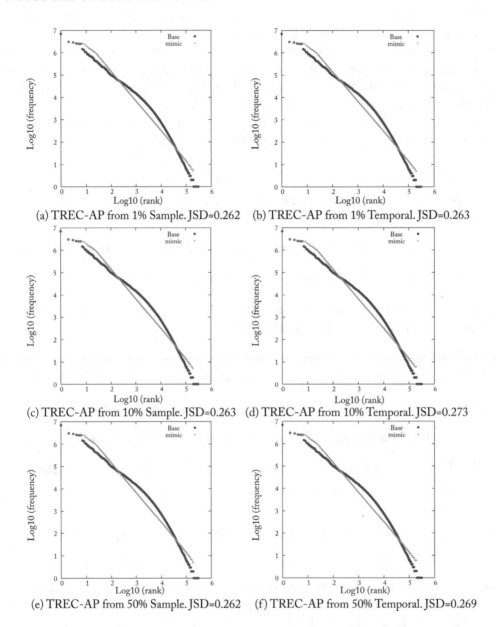

(a) TREC-AP from 1% Sample. JSD=0.262   (b) TREC-AP from 1% Temporal. JSD=0.263

(c) TREC-AP from 10% Sample. JSD=0.263   (d) TREC-AP from 10% Temporal. JSD=0.273

(e) TREC-AP from 50% Sample. JSD=0.262   (f) TREC-AP from 50% Temporal. JSD=0.269

Figure 7.9: Word probability distributions when emulating a full corpus TREC-AP from samples or temporal subsets using corpus-specific growth models and corpusGENERATOR. Plots on the left show scaling up to full size from averaged random samples, while those on the right relate to temporal subsets. Plots for the other temporal growth corpus TREC-WSJ are similar.

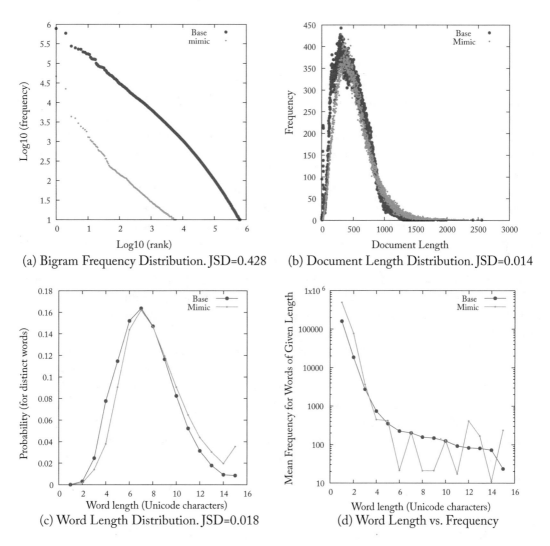

(a) Bigram Frequency Distribution. JSD=0.428

(b) Document Length Distribution. JSD=0.014

(c) Word Length Distribution. JSD=0.018

(d) Word Length vs. Frequency

Figure 7.10: Fidelity of emulation on various dimensions after scaling up 100-fold from 1% samples of the TREC-AP corpus using CORPUSGENERATOR with MARKOV-5E.

An advantage of the string-based Markov method is that the addition of a small amount of noise (λ parameter) can generate words never seen in training.

We trained order-zero and order-one WBMarkov models and a string-based Markov model ($k = 23$, $\lambda = 0.0000025$, $w = 19$) on 1%, 10%, and 50% samples of the corpus and scaled up to the size of the full TREC-AP corpus. Note that we only ran one trial for each condition.

Results and Discussion for Markov Scaling

The graphs in Figure 7.11 compare the ranked word frequency distributions of the scaled-up samples with that of the original. Visually, the plots on the left-hand side suggest that the word-based Markov generators do a good job of matching the word frequency distribution of the original base corpus. However, the logarithmic horizontal scale tends to hide what is a massive deficit in vocabulary size. Careful inspection of the tail of the graphs, particularly the top pair, reveals the absence of many points. Vocabulary sizes are listed in the sub-figure captions, along with JS divergence relative to the ranked word-frequency distribution of the original corpus. The smaller the training sample the greater the vocabulary deficit in the scaled-up result.

The plots for the string-based Markov method on the right-hand side in Figure 7.11 show the beneficial effect of the introduction of noise on the size of the generated vocabulary. The vocabulary size of $\mathbb{B}$ was 308,037. Using a fixed value for lambda resulted in 27% over-generation when scaling up from the 50% sample, and undergeneration by 8% and 31% when scaling up from 10% and 1% samples, respectively. Clearly, the optimum value of λ depends upon the scaling factor. Given a fixed scaling factor it should be possible to tune the value of λ to achieve close to the original vocabulary size.

Figures 7.12 and 7.13 show the fidelity of emulation on other dimensions. Neither word-based nor string-based Markov methods do a good job of emulating the bimodal document length distribution. Unlike WBMarkov0 (plots not shown), both WBMarkov1 and string-MarkovGen with the parameters shown do a good job of matching the bigram frequency distribution. All three methods faithfully emulate the distribution of word lengths (again, WB-Markov0 not shown) although stringMarkovGen produces a small proportion which are truncated at the implementation limit of 15 characters. Interestingly, stringMarkovGen does a much better job of matching the relationship between word length and frequency of occurrence.

7.3   HOW WELL DOES GPT-2 MODEL GROWTH?

As with the Markov generator, the process of word generation in a neural generator is fundamentally a growth model, starting with an empty corpus and growing it until told to stop.

We previously confirmed that the GPT-2 neural generator is able to generate new words not found in the training corpus. This is discussed in Section 6.6.

As noted elsewhere we have used a GPT-2 model to generate synthetic text. We fine-tuned the generic model using the whole of AP. Unfortunately, the slow speed of training and

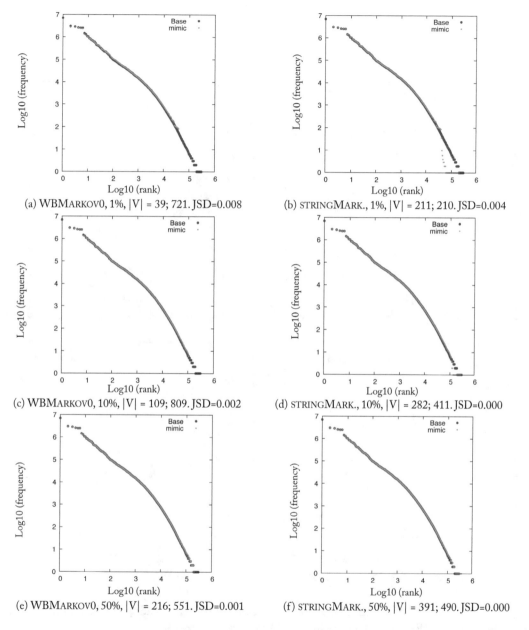

(a) WBMARKOV0, 1%, |V| = 39; 721. JSD=0.008

(b) STRINGMARK., 1%, |V| = 211; 210. JSD=0.004

(c) WBMARKOV0, 10%, |V| = 109; 809. JSD=0.002

(d) STRINGMARK., 10%, |V| = 282; 411. JSD=0.000

(e) WBMARKOV0, 50%, |V| = 216; 551. JSD=0.001

(f) STRINGMARK., 50%, |V| = 391; 490. JSD=0.000

Figure 7.11: Generating full-sized Markov emulations of TREC-AP, after training on samples of different sizes. The left-hand side shows results for order-zero word-based Markov, while the right shows results for string-based Markov with $k = 23, \lambda = 0.0000025, w = 19$. Plots for WBMARKOV1 are virtually identical to those for WBMARKOV0.

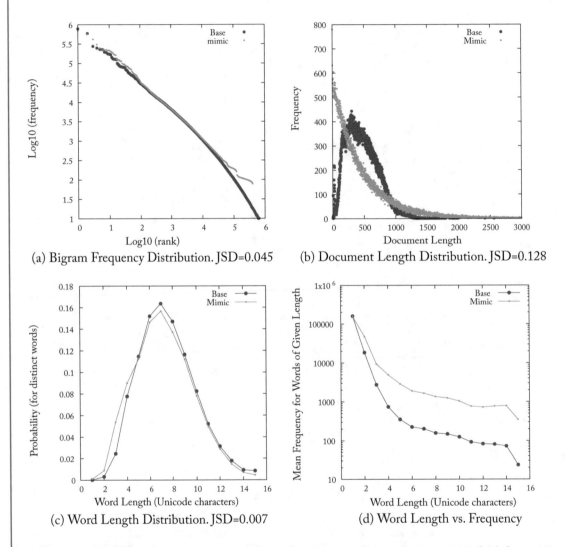

(a) Bigram Frequency Distribution. JSD=0.045

(b) Document Length Distribution. JSD=0.128

(c) Word Length Distribution. JSD=0.007

(d) Word Length vs. Frequency

Figure 7.12: Fidelity of emulation on various dimensions after scaling up 100-fold from 1% samples of the TREC-AP corpus using the WBMARKOV1 method.

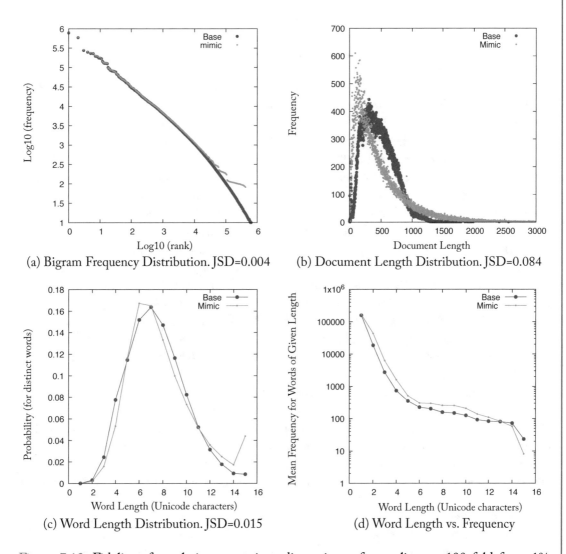

(a) Bigram Frequency Distribution. JSD=0.004   (b) Document Length Distribution. JSD=0.084

(c) Word Length Distribution. JSD=0.015   (d) Word Length vs. Frequency

Figure 7.13: Fidelity of emulation on various dimensions after scaling up 100-fold from 1% samples of the TREC-AP corpus using the STRINGMARKOVGEN method with $k = 23, \lambda = 0.0000025, w = 19$.

generation on the hardware we have available[1] made it impractical to experiment with different training set sizes in time for publication.

7.4   SCALING CONCLUSIONS

Understanding how collections grow is a very interesting topic.[2] We hope that this chapter has shed some useful light.

Of particular interest is the question of whether the samples-from-an-infinite-corpus model is sufficiently accurate for practical purposes. Our experiments suggest that it is. Our experiments with models derived from temporal subsets of a time-ordered (i.e., naturally growing) corpus are hardly definitive but do not show any obvious benefit over the models derived from samples. This is despite the fact that coverage of news topics is inherently bursty. For example, the Fukushima nuclear disaster of March, 2011 caused a temporary rise in the frequency of words such as Fukushima, nuclear, Daiichi, Okuma, meltdowns, reactors etc. in international news media, while the appointment of Brett Kavanaugh to the U.S. Supreme Court in October 2018 caused a temporary rise in frequency of another set of words.

The fundamental practical question is whether scaling up is a useful tool for investigating efficiency and scalability of IR algorithms? The answer is a qualified yes. Clearly scaling up can provide a much more tightly controlled experimental environment than using corpora of different sizes, e.g., studying runtimes on WSJ, GOV, GOV2, and ClueWeb12 corpora. However, if you have a corpus of the largest size you need, such as ClueWeb12, you may be better served by investigating scalability on samples of different sizes. That was the approach taken in the TREC-7 Very Large Collection Track [42], in which 1% and 10% samples were distributed as well as the full VLC2 corpus.

But there are circumstances where experimenters do not have corpora of the maximum size they are interested in. Not everyone has ClueWeb12 and there are private-data scenarios where it is desirable to experiment with corpora larger than the ones to which we have access. For example, an organization has moved some of its document holdings (e.g., those for one office, department, or dataset) to a new platform and plans to eventually migrate all of it. Scaling up allows access to a corpus which is much larger but which shares properties with the subset at hand.

In this chapter we experimented with macro-properties methods, word-based Markov generators, string-based Markov methods, and GPT-2. The macro-properties methods are several orders of magnitude faster than our implementations of Markov and GPT-2 is much slower even than the Markov generators.

A major disadvantage of the word-based Markov generator is that the vocabulary of the scaled-up corpus is no larger than that of the training sample. We found that the string-based

---

[1]HPServer. See Section 1.8.2.

[2]At least to the present authors!

Markov generator overcomes this limitation, but that experimentation with different values of λ may be needed to closely match a desired vocabulary size.

We found that our macro-properties methods were unable to scale up a sample to achieve "perfect" emulation of the original corpus but that the result is likely to be close enough for practical purposes. The biggest limitations arise from the use of a linear rather than piecewise approximation of the middle section of the word frequency distribution and the lack of a growth model for word dependencies.

Our macro-properties experiments were conducted with corpus-specific growth models. In future we plan to experiment with generic growth models learned from multiple corpora.

Another item for future work would be to compare scalability results obtained using real retrieval systems, such as those studied in Chapter 9, on samples of a large corpus with those obtained on scaled-up samples of the same large corpus.

CHAPTER 8

Generation of Compatible Queries

In order to study query processing efficiency and effectiveness using a simulated text corpus, it is necessary to obtain a set of compatible queries and judgments. The text generation methods implemented in SYNTHACORPUS make no pretence of being able to generate meaningful natural language. Consequently, it is presently out of the question that ad hoc queries along the lines of those in the TREC[1] ad hoc task, could be devised or judged.

Baeza-Yates and Navarro [6] discuss methods for random generation of queries, and also for modeling the expected size of the answer sets. Random query sets may be useful for studying throughput and latency of retrieval systems but are not useful for studying retrieval effectiveness. For throughput and latency, we prefer to use translations of real logs; see Section 8.4.

Here we first outline methods for generating pseudo-queries from annotations such as anchortext and explain why these methods are generally not applicable for synthetic corpora. We then present two methods which are applicable and go on to discuss constraints on the emulation of click logs, such as those in the ORCAS data set.

8.1 GENERATING QUERIES FROM DOCUMENT ANNOTATIONS

A number of authors have made use of external textual annotations to develop pseudo query sets applicable in web or enterprise search. Craswell et al. [27] made use of anchor text from an online directory site to generate queries for use in evaluating public web search engines. Hawking et al. [41] used anchortext from the sitemap of Stanford University to compare the performance of Stanford's Google Search Appliance with that of a site-restricted version of the public Google web search service. More recently, a query log derived from anchortext has been used by Dang and Croft [29] to study query reformulation methods.

Pseudo query logs derived from external annotations have also been used in commercial practice. For example, from around 2004, evaluations using queries derived from anchortext and clicked queries were routinely performed by the team behind the Funnelback internet and enterprise search engine.[2]

---

[1]http://trec.nist.gov
[2]https://funnelback.com/. Funnelback was formerly known as P@NOPTIC.

Asadi et al. [1] have used web anchortext to develop a test collection to train learning to rank models. Berendsen et al. have used topic labels [10] and tweets [11] for similar purposes.

Without simulated user interactions, none of the query generation methods based on external textual annotations are available when the document corpus has been simulated. Indeed, non-web corpora have no anchortext. Furthermore, it is frequently the case that the language of annotations differs markedly from the language of queries. For example, a study of one organization by Rowlands [76] found that there were zero exact matches between queries in the log and anchor texts from the site.

8.2   QUERY GENERATION METHODS FOR SYNTHETIC CORPORA

In this chapter we present two alternative methods for generating queries. Azzopardi et al. avoid the need for human judgments by generating known-item queries appropriate to the corpus. Evaluation by known item queries is an established paradigm within the Information Retrieval community, having been used in TREC for retrieval of speech and OCR-ed documents, as well as in the TREC Web Track. The model is that a user has previously seen an interesting document and composes a query in an attempt to re-retrieve it. The challenge for a retrieval system is to retrieve the desired document at the top of the ranked list of results. The methodology of the homepage finding task in the TREC Web track was essentially the same.

We note that the Azzopardi et al. method was extended by Kim and Croft [53] to enable generation of fielded known-item queries.[3] Huurnink et al. [50] also extended it in similar fashion in order to simulate purchase queries from a transaction log of a commercial search engine.

The second method, discussed in Section 8.4, simulates a real stream of queries and may be used to generate realistic loads on a query processing system for efficiency experimentation. It cannot be used for studying effectiveness because human judges would not be able to judge the relevance of randomly generated documents to randomly generated queries.

8.3   AZZOPARDI ET AL. METHOD FOR KNOWN-ITEM QUERIES

Known-item queries allow for effectiveness evaluation in the absence of human judgments. Azzopardi and collaborators [3, 4] have proposed methods for automatic generation of this type of query for real text corpora. In essence, the methods involve randomly selecting a target document and then randomly generating a query which might be used to retrieve it. One of the conclusions of [4] is that achieving good retrieval performance depends upon selecting suitable

---

[3]A fielded query term constrains matching to a specific document field, e.g., `title:simulation` ignores occurrences of `simulation` in parts of a document other than the title.

targets, since humans would be much more likely to select certain documents for re-retrieval than others. They biased target selection toward high-PageRank documents.

SYNTHACORPUS includes a program called QUERYGENERATOR which implements a variant of the method given in Equation 4 of [4]. Given that corpora generated by our methods have no link structure or click information, it is not possible to implement the Azzopardi form of target selection. The algorithm for generating one compatible query is shown in Algorithm 8.2.

Algorithm 8.2 The algorithim implemented by QUERYGENERATOR for generating a known-item query. A candidate target document is considered unsuitable if the number of distinct words it contains is below a threshold T. By default $T = 5$.

1: Randomly pick a target document, making replacement selections if the target(s) are unsuitable.
2: Randomly pick a query length L from a distribution of query lengths.
3: Set the query Q to empty.
4: **for** $w = 1$ to L **do** :
5:     Randomly pick a word W from the document, according to the probabilities given by Azzopardi's Equation 4, and making a replacement selection if the word has already been selected in Q.
6:     Append W to Q.
7: Emit Q.

8.3.1   REPRODUCIBILITY OF KNOWN-ITEM EXPERIMENTS

Experiments using known-item sets generated in this way are eminently reproducible. If a researcher Alice conducts evaluation experiments on an emulated corpus $\mathbb{M}$ using a query set $\mathbb{Q}$ generated by QUERYGENERATOR, another researcher Bob can exactly replicate the experiments, provided that Alice tells Bob the parameters she used when generating $\mathbb{M}$ and $\mathbb{Q}$, including the random seeds.

8.4   MODELING QUERY STREAMS

Simulating the performance of query processing algorithms such as caching requires the use of realistic query arrival sequences. The known-item methods in the previous section do not achieve this. Furthermore, generating queries from the word distribution of the target corpus leads to a different relationship between the word frequency distributions of the query set and the document set.

An alternative approach is illustrated in Figure 8.1. The figure caption explains how the method works. Let us see how the proposed method can achieve accurate emulation.

Word probabilities in the query stream. In the illustration the word `facebook` in the real query stream maps to the word `goeri` in the emulated query stream. Because the same

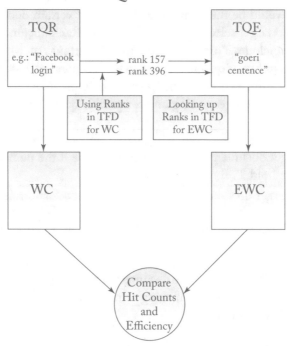

Figure 8.1: Queries from the real query stream TQR are converted word by word into queries in an emulated query stream TQE. A word from a query in TQR is first mapped to its rank r within the word frequency distribution in the real web corpus WC, then the word at rank r in the emulated corpus EWC is emitted. The timings and hit counts when running TQR against WC are then compared with those for running TQE against EWC. If EWC very accurately mimics WC, then the two sets of observations should match each other closely.

mapping is used consistently, the frequency of `goeri` in TQE will inevitably be the same as the frequency of `facebook` in TQR.

Word probabilities in the corpus. The probability of occurrence of the word `facebook` in the real corpus WC may be very different to its probability of occurrence in a query stream. This difference is preserved in the emulated query stream through the mapping via ranks, provided that the word frequency distribution is accurately emulated in EWC.

Word dependence Hit counts and query latency will be affected by co-occurrences between the words comprising a query. If word dependence is not emulated well in EWC, then we would expect there to be significant differences between the running of TQR against WC, and TQE against EWC. Fortunately, in the Synthacorpus approach, word dependency modeling is based on word ranks. If `facebook` and `login` have a significant probability p of co-occurring in WC, then `goeri` and `centence` should co-occur with the same probability in EWC.

This approach may give us a realistic query stream, with realistic hit rates into the target corpus. It can't be used for ranking or effectiveness experiments (no relevance judgments) but it can be used in efficiency experiments, such as comparisons of different caching strategies.

Note that a very similar approach to transforming a query log is presented in [89]. Webber and Moffat replace word w_i in the real query log whose frequency in the real corpus is f with a word from the target (i.e., emulated) corpus which occurs with frequency close to f. They consider a set of candidate substitutions for each word in the query and attempt to make the choices which result in the same co-occurrence frequency for the transformed words in the target corpus as the co-occurrence frequency of the real words in the real corpus. The effectiveness of the co-occurrence method is limited by the need to make consistent choices. If the real query `gun lobby` is transformed to `colorless green`, then the word `gun` appearing in the subsequent real query `elephant gun` must be replaced with `colorless` regardless of whether co-occurrence frequencies can be matched.

If the target corpus were much larger or smaller than the real one, presumably the Webber and Moffat method would be modified to choose according to some function of f rather than f itself.

8.4.1   REPRODUCIBILITY OF EMULATED QUERY STREAM EXPERIMENTS

Allowing another researcher to replicate experiments based on emulated query streams is a little more difficult than in the known-item case. Exact replication would require transfer of the entire emulated query log, and the potential for leakage of confidential information from the original query log would have to be considered.

Let us suppose that researcher Alice in industry proposes a new algorithm for efficient processing of web queries. She validates the algorithm by running a private query stream $\mathbb{Q}$ against a private corpus $\mathbb{B}$. In order to get her paper published she creates an emulated version $\mathbb{M}$ of the corpus and runs an emulated query set $\mathbb{Q}'$ against it, while confirming that the emulated results match the real ones sufficiently well. In order to allow a fellow researcher Bob at another institution (possibly a rival company) to reproduce her results she sends Bob the parameters used to generate $\mathbb{M}$ and includes the random seed so that Bob's version of $\mathbb{M}$ will be identical to hers.

If Alice sends Bob the query set $\mathbb{Q}'$, the volume of data transmitted may be very large[4] and it is possible that Bob, or an adversary Eve, may be able to deduce something about the original query stream.

Another approach which might address both the volume of data and confidentiality concerns, would be for Alice to model $\mathbb{Q}$ as though it were a document collection, using the macro properties methods discussed in preceding chapters—query length model, word fre-

---

[4]Alice could replace the words in $\mathbb{Q}'$ with rank-based term-ids to reduce the dependence on exact replication of $\mathbb{M}$.

quency model, term dependence model, and term representation model. This model could be very compact.

Unfortunately, in a query stream there are dependences across "document" (i.e., query) boundaries. When a searcher reformulates a query, temporally close queries are likely to re-use the same or related words; the distribution of query words at any point in time will depend upon the group of users who are active at that time. Retrieval system features, such as caching, which rely on arrival sequences of queries cannot be usefully studied using a query stream represented in this way. If Alice used the same compact model as Bob, their results would agree but they might not agree with Alice's results obtained on the real data.

8.4.2   CONFIDENTIALITY CONSIDERATIONS

The non-compact form of the emulated query stream can be seen as an encrypted form of the original, where the encryption algorithm is a fixed word-for-word substitution cipher. An adversary Eve may be able to use external information such as expected word frequencies, and likely n-grams to decode at least some of the queries. Eve may be aided by information about the sequence of queries and knowledge of the algorithm used to derive $\mathbb{Q}'$ from $\mathbb{Q}$. This is true even if the words in the emulated query stream are word ranks rather than words. Note that Alice could to some extent defend against this by introducing noise into the process of mapping query words.

To a non-expert eye it seems unlikely, even without the addition of noise, that Eve would succeed in decrypting many of the infrequently occurring words, such as people's names and credit card numbers. The word-for-word encryption might be sufficient to avoid the problems exposed in the AOL query log distribution,[5] which were in any case dramatically magnified by the presence of session identifiers. Session identifiers show the sequences of queries submitted by individuals.

The compact model provides even better protection against attack because it adds randomness to the word mappings and because it removes all vestiges of the original query sequence.

If the query stream contains highly sensitive information such as searches by a chemical company against a patent index, Eve would likely be highly motivated. In this circumstance it would be wise to use the compact model or to avoid sharing even emulated query data.

8.5   SIMULATION OF OTHER QUERY DATASETS

User interactions with web search engines result in the accumulation of vast stores of query-query, document-document, and query-document relationships: Clicks on document D_i retrieved in response to query Q_j can be interpreted as "D_i relevant to Q_j;" clicks on D_i from both Q_j and Q_k (co-clicks) can be interpreted as "semantic relationship between Q_j and Q_k;" clicks on both D_h and D_i from Q_j (another form of co-clicks) can be interpreted as "seman-

---

[5]https://en.wikipedia.org/wiki/AOL_search_data_leak accessed February 23, 2020.

tic relationship between D_h and D_i;" and lexically related Q_k submitted after Q_j in the same session can be interpreted as a reformulation relationship between Q_j and Q_k. Clicks are very useful but may be sparse and are subject to noise.

Space doesn't permit consideration here of other types of user interaction such as dwell time, where a "quick back" can be regarded as a sign of dissatisfaction.

Provided that session data were preserved, the query log emulation method discussed in Section 8.4 would support study of query reformulations at least at the purely lexical level. This is possible because there is a one-to-one mapping between words in $\mathbb{Q}$ and $\mathbb{Q}'$ and because the submission sequence of queries is preserved. However, semantic relationships such as the replacement of of `bulldozer` with `earth moving equipment` would not be modeled.

If the method of Section 8.4 were applied to the queries in a click log containing (query, clicked-URL) pairs, the query-query co-click relationships in the original log would be accurately emulated.

In the next section we discuss the emulation of test collections in which clicks provide the relevance judgments. In this type of collection, the method of Section 8.4 is not sufficient.

8.5.1   TREC DEEP LEARNING TRACK: ORCAS DATASET

ORCAS [26] is a dataset recently released as a resource for the TREC Deep Learning Track. It records 18 million clicks linking 10 million distinct queries with 1.4 million of the TREC DL documents.

In essence, the new collection conforms to the TREC ad hoc model—there is a corpus $\mathbb{B}$ of documents, a set of queries $\mathbb{Q}$, and a set of relevance judgments, in the form of clicks, linking queries in $\mathbb{Q}$ with relevant documents in $\mathbb{B}$.

If we emulated $\mathbb{B}$ using a method which altered the words and retained but altered the URLs, then the emulation of $\mathbb{Q}$ would be highly constrained. For every click $Q_i \rightarrow B_j$ in the original dataset, there would have to be a simulated click $Q'_k \rightarrow M_l$ and the reasons which led to the original click would have to be preserved. In other words, there would need to be the same matching of words between Q'_k and M_l as there was between Q_i and B_j. There would need to be a similar correspondence for the query, URL pairs.

These constraints do not seem to be satisfiable by any of the generator methods we have discussed with the exception of substitution ciphers. If the NOMENCLATOR method[6] were used to emulate $\mathbb{B}$, including URLs, and the same method with the same substitution table were used to emulate the click log including queries and URLs, then the required relationships would be preserved.

Consistent use of NOMENCLATOR encryption would also support the simulation of document-document relationships through co-clicking.

---

[6]See Section 1.5.1.

8.5.2   PRESERVATION OF CONFIDENTIAL INFORMATION

Both NOMENCLATOR and the query log emulation method of Section 8.4 are word substitution ciphers. For discussion of the degree of protection of confidential information of such ciphers, please see Section 8.4.2 and page 142. Note that the meaningful study of the relationships discussed in this section would limit the applicability of the compact-representation and addition-of-noise techniques considered in Section 8.4.2.

8.6   FUTURE WORK: CO-GENERATION OF DOCUMENTS AND QUERIES

We are interested by the idea that, in future, it may be possible to generate documents, queries, and relevance judgments simultaneously. The successful use of language models in information retrieval, where the retriever determines the probability that query and document could have been generated from the same generative model, suggests that this may be possible.

The idea is that if you generate a document d_i and a query q_j from the same topic model, then a retrieval system or a human assessor would be likely to decide that d_i is relevant to q_j, so you can generate a "qrel"[7] linking the two. Furthermore, you could generate a test collection out of many of examples of such (query, document, qrel) triples. There is a risk that a retrieval system might over-fit to the automated process of generating the qrels, but there are ways of mitigating this. A wide range of generative models would be needed, and one would need to have a way of generating partially relevant combinations and red-herrings. Otherwise, the resulting effectiveness task would be too trivial.

Clearly, co-generated test collections wouldn't be sufficient to prove that a retrieval model has good relevance with real users. However, synthetic data could be used to explore the properties of the retrieval model to a far greater extent than might be feasible with real data.

The most likely paths to the co-generation scenario would involve either LDA topic models or deep learning models such as GPT-2.

---

[7]"qrel" is the TREC name given to a relevance judgment between a query and a document.

CHAPTER 9

Proof of the Simulation Pudding

In this chapter, we assess the validity of synthetic test collections, constructed using methods we have described, in IR experimentation. To what extent do the timing, resource usage, and effectiveness results obtainable using synthetic data predict those we would get with real data? We also explore the trade-off between emulation fidelity and confidentiality.

Baeza-Yates and Navarro [6] analyze the effect of document and query models on a block-structured inverted file index. Here our aim is not to compare the efficiency or effectiveness of retrieval systems or methods. Results from our experiments could potentially be used to compare the index structures or ranking algorithms of different systems but we have deliberately avoided looking under the hoods of the retrieval systems. Our goals are to determine whether experiments conducted with simulated collections can sufficiently accurately predict real results, and to compare the fidelity of different emulation methods.

9.1 MAIN EXPERIMENT

9.1.1 METHOD

We use three different IR systems, four TREC corpora, five emulation methods, and several different efficiency and effectiveness measures. If an emulation method were perfect, then the scores on each measure would be the same for the original corpus and for the emulated version. We note that perfection is unlikely and that emulation methods which are close to perfect are likely to entail a high risk of leakage of confidential information from the original data.

Datasets: We chose to use four of our six principal TREC corpora: TREC-AP, TREC-FR, TREC-PAT, and WT10g. Each of them is quite different from the others: Newswire, government, patents, and web pages. As noted in Section 1.8.1, each of these corpora has been converted to UTF-8 and simplified to remove all punctuation and mark-up apart from DOC, DOCNO, and TEXT elements. Table 1.1 summarizes the corpora used.

Using this simple format allows good comparability between measures observed with the base corpus and emulations of it.

Emulation methods: Each of the five emulation methods creates a file in the same simple format as the base corpora. Each emulated corpus was constructed so that it very closely approx-

```
<DOC>
<DOCNO> Doc0 </DOCNO>
<TEXT>
t26362 t368932 t64855 t33466 t044332 t62265 t23046 t78835 t843821
t264032 t23285 t996501 t909682 t221021 t016831 t832522 t885692 t68428
t159031 t98886 t7284 t982411 t327802 t344882 t73642 t685372 t289752
t404341 t5841 t64914 t27763 t674702 t378461 t999731 t847232 t467012
t752122 t614761 t327702 t563871 t73307 t843911 t064941 t802901
...
</TEXT>
</DOC>



<DOC>
<DOCNO> Doc0 </DOCNO>
<TEXT>
crash praisal pi in crash do kamleh ik crash nomadic vauhgan
gimbels crash oo ut boo crash de ux boo crash de ux nev crash
abu iba ma crash xa bogersonellaeg boo crash hob coatham fle
</TEXT>
</DOC>
```

Figure 9.1: Examples of CORPUSGENERATOR-generated text. SIMPLESYNTH is at the top, and SOPHSYNTH at the bottom.

imated the number of documents, word occurrences, and vocabulary size of the corresponding base corpus $\mathbb{B}$.

From among the plethora of possible parameter combinations for CORPUSGENERATOR we choose two: a dumb one with very poor modeling (SIMPLESYNTH) and a sophisticated one which attempts to model the corpus properties very closely (SOPHSYNTH). Example text fragments for each corpus type are given in Figure 9.1. They may be compared with the fragment from the base TREC-AP corpus shown in Figure 1.4.

In SIMPLESYNTH, all the documents have the same length (the average length in $\mathbb{B}$) and the word frequency distribution is uniform, i.e., all words have the same frequency. Words in this emulated corpus comprise the letter "t" and a number. There is no modeling of compound terms.

In SOPHSYNTH, the documents have the same lengths as in $\mathbb{B}$, and the word frequency distribution quite accurately models that of $\mathbb{B}$. The frequencies of the ten most frequent words are explicitly the same as in $\mathbb{B}$, the number of singletons is explicitly modeled and the frequencies of other words are piecewise modeled with ten segments. n-gram frequencies up to three words are modeled.

Table 9.1: Open source IR systems used in our study

System	Downloaded	Language	IR Model	URL
ATIRE	28 May, 2019	C++	BM25	http://atire.org/
Indri	29 May, 2019	C++	Default LM	https://github.com/diazf/indri
Terrier	14 June, 2019	Java	DFR	http://terrier.org/download/

We also study two cryptographic emulation methods to shed light on the trade-off between emulation fidelity and privacy loss: Caesar1 and Nomenclator, described in Section 1.5.1. For Nomenclator, the vocabulary generated in the SophSynth emulation of a corpus is used as the cipher vocabulary. Words from the base corpus are randomly mapped to words from the SophSynth emulation, generated using the markov-5e method.

Note: As implemented, the Caesar1 method only deals with ASCII letters. That isn't a problem for TREC-AP, TREC-FR, TREC-PAT, but means that some text in WT10g is not encrypted. We decided that this is very unlikely to affect results or conclusions.

Finally, to allow us to observe the effects of file system layout on physical storage (hard disk or SSD) we also study the Cp method which emulates by making a byte-for-byte copy of 𝔹. Any differences in timing between Cp and Base versions of a corpus set an upper bound on the fidelity which can be achieved by any real emulation method.

Queries and judgments: Emulations generally do not permit the use of query sets or judgments pertaining to the base corpus. Accordingly, we use the variant of the Azzopardi et al. method described in Section 8.3, for generating known-item queries: Randomly pick a target document and generate a query intended to retrieve it. We use sets of a thousand queries. Within a set the lengths are distributed according to a left-truncated normal distribution whose standard deviation is half of the specified mean. Whenever an emulated corpus is generated (and once for each Base corpus) we generate three corresponding query sets with mean lengths of three, six, and nine words.

IR Systems: We used three different publicly available IR systems which are listed in Table 9.1. Each of them supports multiple retrieval methods but we chose a single different method for each.

The aim of the experiment is not to compare retrieval systems but to investigate whether their efficiency/effectiveness performance on a base corpus can be predicted by their performance on an emulated one. However, we did consult with the maintainers of the three systems about the best configuration settings for our hardware configuration. Indri was compiled without optimization because it failed when compiled with -O3 on the Macintosh LLVM compiler.[1]

---

[1]https://llvm.org/

Hardware: The experiment was run on the OldMac system.[2] It was not disconnected from the network, nor run in single-user mode. However, during the experiment user applications were shut down, and the machine was not used for other purposes. The implementation of the IR systems (using default settings) determined whether use was made of the laptop's four physical cores, or only one.

The experiment (including extracting properties, and generating corpora and query sets) took three and a half days to run.

Measures: Our primary measure is *prediction accuracy ratio* R_1, described in Section 2.1.

We used eight underlying measures: elapsed time to process a query set; mean reciprocal rank (MRR) for each of the three query sets; elapsed time to index the data; and memory required for indexing. The last of these measures was recorded only for ATIRE which produces it by default.

When aggregating measures across corpora or across retrieval systems or both, averaging underlying primary measures makes no sense. It's obviously invalid to average across different scales of measurement such as time and mean reciprocal rank. However, it is valid to average prediction accuracies in all these cases. Furthermore, even averaging across times would be fraught with problems because times for some corpora and some retrieval systems would totally dominate times for the others.

We used the TREC_EVAL program version 9.0 downloaded from NIST https://trec.nist.gov/trec_eval/ on June 13, 2019 to calculate MRR scores.

Key details of the experiment: Every timing measurement was repeated five times, while MRR scores were calculated once per condition.

For the deterministic methods (Cp, Caesar1, and Nomenclator) one emulation of each corpus was performed. For each of the non-deterministic SynthaCorpus methods five different emulations of each Base corpus were made using different random seeds. Accordingly, $5 \times 5 = 25$ timing observations were made for each of the SophSynth and SimpleSynth emulation methods, for each different corpus. For each new emulation (not for each trial with the same corpus) new query sets were generated.

Each combination of corpus and query set was processed by each of the IR systems. For example, the second SophSynth emulation of the TREC-AP corpus and its associated query sets was processed five times by each of ATIRE, Indri, and Terrier.

9.1.2   RESULTS

In all of the box and whisker plots in this section, the vertical axis represents prediction accuracy R_1, the boxes represent the middle two quartiles and the ends of the whiskers represent the extreme values of the scores. The green points shown in some plots represent the arithmetic mean of the prediction accuracies for each condition. We connect the means with lines to improve clarity. The horizontal axis contains one or more groups. In each group the emulation meth-

---

[2]See Section 1.8.2

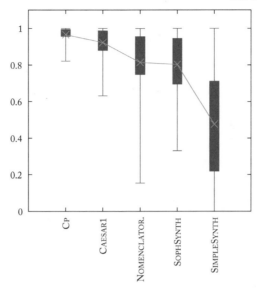

Figure 9.2: R_1 scores across *all the measures*, all the retrieval systems, all the query lengths, and all the corpora.

ods are ordered left to right in expected order of decreasing prediction accuracy: CP, CAESAR1, NOMENCLATOR, SOPHSYNTH, SIMPLESYNTH.

Overall comparison of emulation methods: Figure 9.2 displays the R_1 scores across all the measures, all the retrieval systems, all the query lengths, and all the corpora. The number of observations represented for each of the deterministic methods (leftmost three) is 296. For each of the others the number of observations is 1480.

The mean R_1 shows a decline from left to right across the emulation methods, with a sharp drop for SIMPLESYNTH. The means from left to right are 0.964, 0.922, 0.813, 0.802, and 0.476. It is quite encouraging that the two methods which might conceivably be used in practice (NOMENCLATOR and SOPHSYNTH) achieve very similar mean R_1 scores, each above 0.8. In the measure by measure analysis which follows, we see that the means for these two methods are very similar for each measure except indexing memory.

The whiskers on the plots show some quite extreme values which we will discuss when we consider individual measures. The variations in R_1 for the CP method may be due to differences in query sets generated by the random process and to measurement noise—variation in time due to disk layout or operating system vagaries. Analysis shows that all of the R_1 values for CP below 0.96 relate to query processing time, the dimension most likely to be affected by differences in query sets. We conclude that the contribution of measurement noise is only a few percent.

Overall comparisons on a per measure basis: Figures 9.3–9.6 compare the emulation methods on one measure at a time, to examine if predictions are better for some measures than others.

The plot of indexing time shows a very similar pattern to the overall one, but the range of values is substantially reduced. SIMPLESYNTH performs very poorly. With it, ATIRE takes up to 8.5 times as long to index an emulated corpus as the corresponding Base. The opposite is true for Terrier, where the emulated corpora are indexed much faster than Base. Indri shows a wide spread in R_2 ratios, from 1.4 for TREC-AP to 5.1 for WT10g. Since we are only interested in comparing simulation methods, we haven't tried to explain the effect of SIMPLESYNTH on the performance of the retrieval systems.

We only obtained indexing memory data for the ATIRE retrieval system. The small variations shown in Figure 9.4 are thus due to differences between corpora. SOPHSYNTH and SIMPLESYNTH show encouragingly small variation, given that they include results for five different emulations of each corpus. The R_1 scores for SOPHSYNTH are much less than those for NOMENCLATOR. This observation is unexpected as, on other measures those two methods generally make similarly accurate predictions.

Query processing time (Figure 9.5) shows a greater degree of variability than for either of the indexing measures, no doubt due to the variation between randomly generated query sets. SOPHSYNTH and SIMPLESYNTH each include data for fifteen different query sets per corpus which probably explains their considerable variability. The very large range for NOMENCLATOR is more surprising, since there are only three query sets per corpus. Detailed analysis shows that all the R_1 values below 0.25 for NOMENCLATOR relate to the TREC-PAT corpus and the ATIRE retrieval system.

Query processing accuracy (Figure 9.6) shows a very different picture. All emulation methods, except for SIMPLESYNTH, permit very good predictions of the mean reciprocal rank obtained on the base corpus; SIMPLESYNTH achieves a reasonable mean of 0.629 but shows a huge spread of values indicative of some very poor predictions. Detailed analysis showed 160 cases where either Indri or Terrier, on SIMPLESYNTH emulations, achieved less than 10% of the reciprocal rank score they achieved on the Base corpus.

Per retrieval system comparisons: We investigated whether the ability of an emulation method to make good predictions was dependent on the retrieval system. Figure 9.7 shows the results for each of the three retrieval systems. The five bars on the left relate to ATIRE, the middle five to Indri and the rest to Terrier.

There does appear to be an interaction between emulation method and retrieval system. Ignoring the results for SIMPLESYNTH, predictions are generally very accurate for Indri, quite accurate for Terrier, and quite variable for ATIRE. Investigation of low scores for ATIRE. SOPHSYNTH shows that processing of three word queries by ATIRE took at least 2.7 times as long for the SOPHSYNTH emulation of WT10g in all 25 observations.

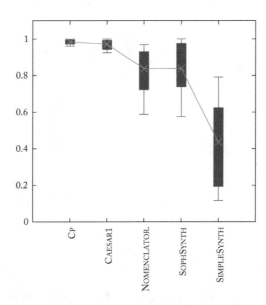

Figure 9.3: R_1 scores for *indexing time* across all the retrieval systems and all the corpora.

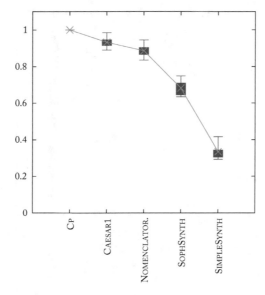

Figure 9.4: R_1 scores for *indexing memory* across all the corpora.

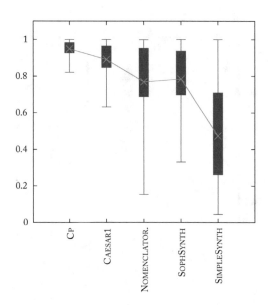

Figure 9.5: R_1 scores for *query processing time* across all the retrieval systems, all the query lengths, and all the corpora.

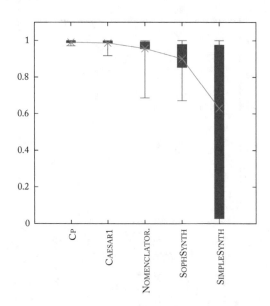

Figure 9.6: R_1 scores for *mean reciprocal rank* across all the retrieval systems, all the query lengths, and all the corpora.

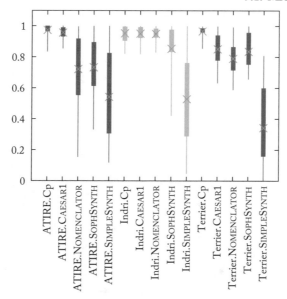

Figure 9.7: R_1 scores *per retrieval system*, across all the measures, all the query lengths, and all the corpora.

Per corpus comparisons: We made a similar study of a possible interaction between emulation method and corpus. Figure 9.8 shows the results for each of the four corpora. Proceeding from left to right, the groups of five bars represent TREC-AP, TREC-FR, TREC-PAT, and WT10g corpora. We see many differences across corpora. Some salient differences include: Better accuracy for SOPHSYNTH on TREC-AP than on the other corpora; very poor accuracy of SIMPLESYNTH on WT10g.

Further results for indexing memory: Being able to predict the memory requirements of a production IR system may be quite important for hardware sizing. We present in Table 9.2 the ratios for the memory requirements reported by the ATIRE indexer. Ratios increase from left to right across every row. SIMPLESYNTH is associated with very bad prediction accuracy while CP unsurprisingly makes perfect predictions. It is not clear why CAESAR1 does not also make perfect predictions since all parameters are the same, including word lengths and the relationship between word length and word frequency. As noted earlier, we are also surprised that the memory requirements for SOPHSYNTH are consistently greater than those for NOMENCLATOR. This is particularly surprising since the lexicon for both is the same, i.e., the list of words is the same but the frequencies are different.

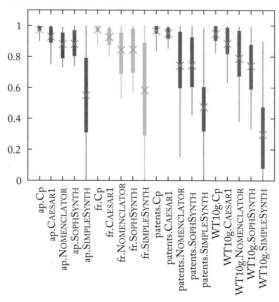

Figure 9.8: R_1 scores *per corpus*, averaged across all the measures, all the query lengths, and all the retrieval systems.

Table 9.2: Emulation to Base (R_2) ratios for the indexing memory requirement reported by ATIRE for each emulation method across four corpora

Corpus.System	CP	CAESAR1	NOMENCLATOR	SOPH.SYNTH	SIMPLE.SYNTH
ap.ATIRE	1.000	1.123	1.127	1.332	2.404
fr.ATIRE	1.000	1.102	1.243	1.432	2.945
patents.ATIRE	1.000	1.015	1.058	1.399	3.137
WT10g.ATIRE	1.000	1.072	1.200	1.527	3.246
Column means	1.000	1.078	1.157	1.423	2.933

9.1.3 DISCUSSION OF MAIN EXPERIMENT

The small variation in observations for the CP method, including for retrieval accuracy, suggest that there is acceptably small noise in the results. We believe that most of that noise is due to the random generation of query sets.

CAESAR1 is another straw method. Because it provides no practical protection for confidential information, there would be no point in using it in practice. It is interesting that indexing time is slightly slower than for CP and shows greater variability, and that ATIRE uses slightly more memory during indexing CAESAR1 than during indexing CP. The fact that query processing time is slower for CAESAR1 than for CP, is probably due to query set differences, though retrieval accuracy for the two methods is very similar.

The SIMPLESYNTH method, in which each of the words in the vocabulary are assumed to occur an equal number of times, is unsurprisingly associated with very bad prediction accuracy. It was included to explore the extent of the prediction errors caused by using a very poor emulation method. Bad as it is, SIMPLESYNTH is not as bad as it could be since it generates the same number of word occurrences as in the Base corpus, and creates a vocabulary of the same size.

Overall, we conclude that measurements taken from corpora emulated by the methods which could be conceivably be used in practice (NOMENCLATOR and SOPHSYNTH) are capable of predicting some real-world measurements, such as indexing and query processing speed, and memory requirements, with enough accuracy to be practically useful. Although predictions of query processing accuracy made from NOMENCLATOR and SOPHSYNTH are very good, it is not clear yet whether corpora emulated with these methods would be sufficient to meaningfully perform tuning of a retrieval system, or to guide purchase of a search engine to operate on a private corpus.

Failure to model term burstiness in the corpusGENERATOR methods is likely to contribute to lower prediction accuracy since, without it, match sets will tend to be larger and relevance signals weaker. Implementing term burstiness should be a priority for SYNTHACORPUS development.

It would be interesting to understand the variation in prediction accuracy across corpora shown in Figure 9.8. Our initial thought was that simulation of homogeneous corpora (such as TREC-AP) might be easier since SIMPLESYNTH and SOPHSYNTH essentially generate all documents from the same model, rather than from a mixture of models. However, prediction accuracy for NOMENCLATOR also varies across the corpora, and it very faithfully models the diversity of documents in a corpus. This issue remains open for future investigation.

SIMPLESYNTH and SOPHSYNTH illustrate how the macro-properties methods can be used to engineer corpora with very different properties. We claim that varying the parameters of corpusGENERATOR in more targeted ways or using other emulation methods within SYNTHACORPUS could be a useful way of studying the performance of retrieval systems. The interactions between retrieval system and emulation method, presented above, indicate that there may be benefit from such explorations.

Apart from SIMPLESYNTH, all methods do an exceptionally good job of predicting mean reciprocal rank scores (see Figure 9.6). CAESAR1, NOMENCLATOR, and SOPHSYNTH do almost as well as CP. This level of prediction accuracy is perhaps surprising since the query sets are necessarily different between $\mathbb{M}$ and $\mathbb{B}$. We suspect that our necessary modification of the Azzopardi et al. query generation method produces queries which are too discriminating, i.e., that the retrieval task is too easy.

One caveat associated with the corpusGENERATOR emulations is that the particular corpus generated is dependent on a sequence of random numbers. Controlling for this may require generating a much higher number of emulated corpora for each CORPUSGENERATOR condition than we used in the main experiment. We addressed this in a follow-up.

9.2   FOLLOW-UP EXPERIMENTS

In this section we describe two follow-ups from the main experiment. The first is an investigation into variation in measurements taken from the CORPUSGENERATOR methods due to different random number sequences. The second is to present some results for emulation methods which were not feasible to include in the main experiment.

9.2.1   VARIATION DUE TO CHOICE OF RANDOM SEED

Unless told to use a fixed random seed, multiple runs of the SynthaCorpus corpus generator will result in different corpora, even when exactly the same parameters are given. Dfferent corpora will yield different values for times and MRR scores and, of course, different prediction accuracy values. In the experiment we have just described, we attempted to control for this source of variation, by basing each data point for the SynthaCorpus methods on five different emulated corpora. For each timing measure on each emulated corpus we took the mean of five observations to control for measurement noise due to timing inaccuracy and possible process contention due to extraneous activities such as email arrival or operating system housekeeping.

We wanted to understand how much variability in prediction accuracy arises from the choice of random seed in the corpus generator. However, on the computing hardware available, it took days to run the experiment described in this section. Therefore, it was not practical to rerun it with a much higher number of emulations per corpus. We, therefore, explored this source of variation for a single corpus and for only the SOPHSYNTH emulation method while increasing the number of emulations to 30. We also report variation in R_2 ratios.

Results are presented in Tables 9.3–9.5. They show that the standard deviations of the distribution of R_1 values over 30 different corpora are no greater than 5% of the means—much less than that for many of the measures. The mean R_2 values show an interesting anomaly in Table 9.4. It is unclear why the prediction of Indri query processing time is so poor.

In summary, the variation in predictions due to choice of random seed seems acceptably small.

9.2.2   FOLLOW-UP 2: EVALUATION OF GPT-2 AND MARKOV METHODS

Because of the slow generation rates for the GPT-2 and high-order Markov methods, it was not feasible to include those methods in the main experiment. We therefore ran a cut-down version of the main experiment using just one emulation of the TREC-AP corpus for each of four emulation methods. We present prediction ratios for each retrieval system in Table 9.6.

Looking at the mean R_2 ratio, it appears that GPT-2 can make very accurate predictions. Its mean R_2 ratio is closest to 1. However, this is because some of the individual R_2 ratios are

Table 9.3: Variation in R_1 and R_2 for indexing time. G is the number of different emulated corpora generated by the SOPHSYNTH method. The standard deviations are no greater than 2.5% of the means. Runs were performed on NewMac with minimal other activity.

Condition	R_2		R_1		
	Mean	Standard Deviation	Mean	Standard Deviation	G
ap.ATIRE.SophSynth.it	1.1698	0.0289	0.8553	0.0189	30
ap.Indri.SophSynth.it	0.9890	0.0081	0.9887	0.0076	30
ap.Terrier.SophSynth.it	1.0906	0.0271	0.9175	0.0229	30

Table 9.4: Variation in R_1 and R_2 for time to process a batch of 1000 6-word known-item queries. The standard deviations are no greater than 5% of the means. Runs were performed on NewMac with minimal other activity.

Condition	R_2		R_1		
	Mean	Standard Deviation	Mean	Standard Deviation	G
ap.ATIRE.SophSynth.q6t	1.2081	0.0314	0.8283	0.0215	30
ap.Indri.SophSynth.q6t	2.3016	0.1082	0.4354	0.0203	30
ap.Terrier.SophSynth.q6t	1.1239	0.0280	0.8903	0.0223	30

Table 9.5: Variation in R_1 and R_2 for reciprocal rank averaged over a batch of 1000 6-word known-item queries. The standard deviations are no more than 0.5% of the means. Runs were performed on NewMac with minimal other activity.

Condition	R_2		R_1		
	Mean	Standard Deviation	Mean	Standard Deviation	G
ap.ATIRE.SophSynth.q6rr	1.0257	0.0049	0.9750	0.0046	30
ap.Indri.SophSynth.q6rr	1.0227	0.0051	0.9779	0.0048	30
ap.Terrier.SophSynth.q6rr	1.0393	0.0055	0.9623	0.0051	30

greater than 1 and others are less than 1. This illustrates why it's most useful to use R_1 ratios when averaging across conditions.

Ranking the methods by their mean R_1 we see that SIMPLESYNTH performs quite poorly and has a high variance. STRINGMARKOV/15, WBMARKOV1, and SOPHSYNTH perform best, and very similarly to each other, with quite small variance. GPT-2 performs much better than SIMPLESYNTH but one standard deviation below the top performer.

Table 9.6: Overall performance prediction accuracy ratios for emulation of the TREC-AP corpus. Ratios are the means of prediction accuracies derived from primary measures averaged over ten observations each for each of the retrieval systems ATIRE, Indri, and Terrier. (Two extreme outliers were removed from the indexing times for Terrier.) Parameters for STRING-MARKOV/5 were $k = 5, w = 0, \lambda = 0$. Parameters for STRINGMARKOV/15 were $k = 15, w = 13, \lambda = 0.000006$. In both STRINGMARKOV cases, the Markov alphabet comprised only case-folded ASCII letters plus end-of-document, end-of-sentence, and end-of-word symbols. Runs were done on NewMac with minimal other activity.

Condition	R_2		R_1	
	Mean	Standard Deviation	Mean	Standard Deviation
SIMPLESYNTH	1.1019	1.2839	0.5825	0.3507
GPT-2	0.9774	0.2788	0.8121	0.1425
STRINGMARKOV/5	1.0201	0.1992	0.8854	0.1179
SOPHSYNTH	1.1163	0.1748	0.8958	0.1063
WBMARKOV1	1.1260	0.1418	0.9004	0.0980
STRINGMARKOV/15	1.0907	0.1440	0.9094	0.0926

9.3   EMULATING AUTHOR STYLE

For emulations resulting in similar vocabulary to the base corpus, it is reasonable to consider to what extent $\mathbb{M}$ matches the writing style of $\mathbb{B}$.

Author attribution (Did Shakespeare really write *Hamlet*?) has been the subject of a considerable amount of research, and public interest. A recent book by Savoy [78] describes a number of methods for measuring the stylistic distance between one text and another. Here we present the results of a small experiment using the stylistic distance measure due to Labbé [56]. The distance is calculated by summing the absolute differences between the frequencies of the t most common words in each text, and dividing by the overall total of those frequencies. The Labbé distance can range between 0 (identical) and 1 (no overlap).

Our experiment used only the STRINGMARKOVGEN method. We were interested to see how the Labbé distance between $\mathbb{M}$ and $\mathbb{B}$ varied as the order k of the model increased. We used the Robert Louis Stevenson texts from the Oxquarry1 corpus defined by Ledger [58] and used in both [56] and [78]. On the assumption that Associated Press has a house style we also performed various emulations of the TREC-AP corpus. We set $t = 200$ and calculated the distance for the top t bigrams as well as the top t words.

Figure 9.9 shows the results. As expected, small values of k result in poor emulation of the style of the original. However, as k increases, the stylistic distances decrease virtually to zero.

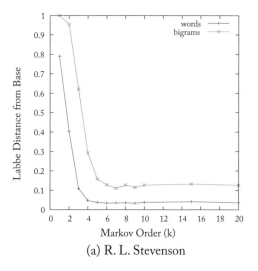

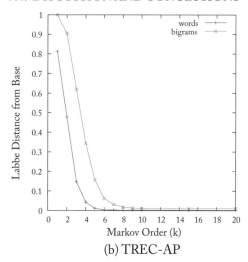

(a) R. L. Stevenson

(b) TREC-AP

Figure 9.9: The effect of k on the ability of STRINGMARKOVGEN to emulate the writing style of an author and a newswire service.

The reason that style emulation is better for TREC-AP than for Stevenson may well be due to the very much greater volume of data in TREC-AP.

9.4 DISCUSSION AND CONCLUSIONS

In Section 9.1.3, we claimed that the NOMENCLATOR and SOPHSYNTH methods were able to make predictions sufficiently accurate for use in practice. We pointed out that the emulated corpus generated by the SOPHSYNTH method was determined by a random number generator and that the sample of five emulations for each condition might not be sufficient. We addressed that in a follow-up experiment where we increased the number of emulations to 30 and observed mean and standard deviation of both the R_1 and R_2 ratios. Results suggested that the variation due to random seed was acceptably small.

In a second follow-up experiment, we assessed the performance of the neural method GPT-2 and high order Markov methods against SOPHSYNTH and SIMPLESYNTH methods. We found that STRINGMARKOV/15, WBMARKOV1, and SOPHSYNTH were the best of those methods but due to the necessarily limited scope of the experiment these conclusions must be regarded as tentative.

We conclude that NOMENCLATOR and SOPHSYNTH emulate corpus properties sufficiently well to be considered in applications relating to confidential corpora, at least for the purposes of technology evaluation and hardware capacity planning. However, further refinement of the method for generating known item queries would likely bring benefits in the form of better discrimination between ranking algorithms.

Although GPT-2 and high-order Markov methods seem to more accurately model linguistic structures than SOPHSYNTH, these advantages are offset by slower speed and probable proneness to information leakage.

CHAPTER   10

Speed of Operation

In this chapter we take a look at the speed of operation of various components of the SYNTHA-CORPUS suite. We start with a somewhat off-the-wall idea, that of building a text generator into the retrieval system component (particularly the indexer) in order to save on the time and space needed to write very large corpora to disk.

10.1   ON-THE-FLY TEXT GENERATION

A simple SYNTHACORPUS model can provide a very compact representation of a huge volume of text. If the generative model is small enough, and one is studying a process, such as indexing, which requires a single pass through a vast dataset, it might be possible to generate the text on the fly. For example, instead of requesting the next word from disk, an indexer might call a generator to create the next word according to the model. This could potentially save terabytes of space on disk, and hours of processing to generate the files on disk according to the model.

For this approach to provide meaningful estimates of processing time, the memory and CPU requirements of the internal word (and document boundary) generator should be comparable with those of reading the same amount of data off disk or SSD. Otherwise the rate of processing will be slowed by CPU and/or cache contention.

We experimented with building a generator into an indexer used inside Microsoft but found that, to avoid slowing down indexing, we were restricted to very simple models. The methods we envisaged for modeling n-gram distributions, term co-occurrence (including self co-occurrence) and text representation of words, were not compatible with the CPU and cache restrictions. To implement the on-the-fly scenario with these methods would require running the corpus generator on a separate server. It seems to us unlikely that there would be many applications where that approach would be preferable to writing the corpus to disk prior to experimentation.

10.2   SPEED OF GENERATION

Even excluding on-the-fly generation scenarios, the speed of generation of text is an important consideration when the generated corpus is very large. A back-of-the-envelope calculation (multiplying the number of indexable words per web page in WT10g by the 733 million web pages in ClueWeb12) suggests that the number of word occurrences (postings) in ClueWeb12 is about 450 billion. A generator operating at one million postings per second would take about five days to generate a corpus of that size. At 1000 postings per second it would take 5000 days or nearly 14 years.

Of course, generation could be run in parallel using many CPUs. However, many of the generation algorithms are not cache friendly, meaning that achieving good parallel speed-up would require that the CPUs did not share RAM. That effectively rules out taking significant advantage of multiple cores on a single chip.

Speed of query generation is of some concern since evaluation of query processing latency and effectiveness benefits from test sets containing millions, even billions, of queries. However, it is less critical than speed of corpus generation since the volumes of data are very much smaller.

Running a query submitter on a server separate from the query processing system is established practice in industry. Such a query submitter is able to model the query arrival rates and patterns expected at times of peak load and can be used to stress test the retrieval engine. A useful query submitter based on the Azzopardi algorithm could be built if the implementation were fast enough.

10.3 SPEED EXPERIMENTS

In this section we show how speed of text generation (measured in word occurrences per second) varies with the degree of sophistication of the models used in generation, and with the size of the generated corpus. We also looked at the time taken to extract properties from a real corpus. Unless otherwise stated, all speed experiments were run single-threaded on OldMac (see Section 1.8.2).

10.3.1 PROPERTY EXTRACTION SPEED

The process used by CORPUSPROPERTYEXTRACTOR to extract the properties necessary for COR-PUSGENERATOR to emulate a base corpus or to provide the basis for scaling up is relatively straightforward, all except for the extraction of compound terms, specifically n-grams. The code for extracting significant n-grams involves putting all the candidates into a large hash table. If document D_i comprises $|d_i|$ word occurrences, then $|d_i| - 1$ bigrams, $|d_i| - 2$ trigrams, and so on, are inserted into the hash table for that document. Huge numbers of distinct n-grams are inserted into the table but most of them occur so infrequently that they do not qualify for significance. In the absence of pruning, the hash table potentially becomes too large for primary memory, and page thrashing ensues. Even with heuristics to prune the very low-frequency candidates when the table becomes close to full, the whole process is time consuming.

To convey an approximate idea of the time taken, extracting properties from WT10g takes about **4.5 minutes** on OldMac when n-grams are not recorded, about **7.7 minutes** when 2-grams are recorded, and about **19.1 minutes** when both 2- and 3-grams are recorded.

10.3.2   CORPUS GENERATION SPEED

Table 10.1 reports generation times and rates of generation for a number of different emulation methods. The times and rates include the time taken to train models (if applicable). In the case of SophSynth the training time relates to the size of the vocabulary which grows more slowly than the size of the corpus, and the rate of generation increases with the size of the corpus. SimpleSynth is almost 50 times faster than SophSynth on T8 NLQs but less than twice as fast on TREC-AP.

GPT-2: To generate the GPT-2 collection we fine-tuned the 774 million parameter model with the TREC-AP collection. For this we used a single CPU of HPServer (see Section 1.8.2). We trained for about 18,000 steps with each step taking about 20 sec, resulting in an average cross-entropy loss of about 2.5. We generated the documents on the same machine, but on the K80 GPUs, running the model on each of the 2 GPUs in parallel, with a batch_size of 14 (thereby utilizing as much of each GPU's memory as possible). Each document took about 5.76 sec to generate, thus producing about 80.7 postings per second.

It is clear that the GPT-2 method is orders of magnitude slower than the other methods we have considered, even after the model has been trained and fine-tuned. The time required for training and fine-tuning is considerable and likely to dwarf the run time of the model.

For the five methods which might be considered for use in practice (NOMENCLATOR, SophSynth, WBMarkov1, stringMarkovGen, and GPT-2) the approximate rates of generation during emulation of TREC-AP are, respectively: **4**, **5**, **1**, **0.3**, and **0.0001** million word occurrences per second. However, considerable variation of times was observed. Consequently, the generation rates should be considered as indicative only.

10.3.3   GENERATING VERY LARGE CORPORA

We'd like to confirm the ability of corpusGenerator to generate corpora of the scale of ClueWeb12. However a single SophSynth run producing 450 billion word occurrences would take of the order of 2.5 days, based on the data for WT10g in Table 10.1. Maintaining that rate requires that the intermediate array be largely kept in RAM during shuffling. The array has 450 billion entries, each of 4 bytes, giving a RAM requirement of at least 1.8 terabytes. The large machine mentioned in Section 1.8.2 has more than enough RAM for this, but we didn't try to confirm the feasibility. With current technology, it seems almost inevitable that a retrieval system working on close to a billion documents would partition the corpus across many servers.

Accordingly, it would make sense to generate a full ClueWeb12-sized corpus in partitions, perhaps by performing the generation on multiple servers. We envisage a system in which ClueWeb12 would be split into 15 partitions, each of roughly 50 million documents or 30 billion word occurrences. An interesting theoretical issue arises—how to create appropriate sub-vocabularies in each of the partitions.

Since queries will be processed by the retrieval system across all of the partitions in parallel, we should think of a shared overall vocabulary of which each partition uses a subset.

Table 10.1: Speed of generation for a number of generation methods while emulating different corpora. Apart from GPT-2, times were averaged over three runs on OldMac with minimal competing workload, and training times are included. For GPT-2 there was only one run, using the GPUs on HPServer, and training times are not included. (*Continues.*)

Method	Time to Generate (sec.)	Rate (Mwords/sec.)
Baseline	0.272	4.503
Caesar1	0.188	6.526
Cp	0.044	27.916
WBMarkov0	0.923	1.329
WBMarkov1	1.317	0.931
stringMarkovGen $k = 9$	2.165	0.567
Nomenclator	0.969	1.265
SimpleSynth	0.131	9.336
SophSynth	5.010	0.245
(a) T8 NLQs: 1.23M Postings		

Method	Time to Generate (sec.)	Rate (Mwords/sec.)
Baseline	13.238	8.542
Caesar1	4.439	25.471
Cp	1.746	64.779
WBMarkov0	38.615	2.928
WBMarkov1	106.018	1.067
stringMarkovGen $k = 9$	339.609	0.333
Nomenclator	28.200	4.010
SimpleSynth	14.461	7.819
SophSynth	23.557	4.800
GPT-2	500 hr.s	0.000087
(b) TREC-AP: 113.1M Postings		

Table 10.1: (*Continued.*) Speed of generation for a number of generation methods while emulating different corpora. Apart from GPT-2, times were averaged over three runs on OldMac with minimal competing workload, and training times are included. For GPT-2 there was only one run, using the GPUs on HPServer, and training times are not included.

Method	Time to Generate (sec.)	Rate (Mwords/sec.)
BASELINE	165.131	6.281
CAESAR1	42.221	24.565
CP	20.900	49.624
STRINGMARKOVGEN $k = 9$	6559.675	0.158
NOMENCLATOR	272.090	3.826
SIMPLESYNTH	213.198	4.865
SOPHSYNTH	489.785	2.118
(c) WT10g: 1037.2M Postings		

If we independently run 15 SOPHSYNTH generators, each producing a partition of 30 billion word occurrences, we will not get what we want. The use of different random number sequences will mean that the word strings in the lexicons of the different partitions will be different. Even if that can be solved by sharing a random seed, the size of the union vocabulary across the partitions will be just the maximum across the partitions, much smaller than the size expected by the Heaps/Herdan law.

Working out how to modify CORPUSGENERATOR to do the right thing in the case of partitioned corpora remains for future work.

In future work, we propose to gauge how large a corpus could be emulated without loss of speed due to paging, using SOPHSYNTH on a single machine with 64 GB of RAM (e.g., NewMac). If a process were able to keep resident 60 billion bytes of intermediate array, i.e., 15 billion 4-byte integers, that would suggest a limit of 15 billion postings in a single corpus. However, the locality of reference pattern of the Durstenfeld algorithm is much better than random scatter. We hope that it might be possible to achieve reasonable generation rates for 20 or even 30 billion word occurrences, the latter being the approximate size of ClueWeb12 Category B.

10.3.4   QUERY GENERATION SPEED

The time taken to generate known-item queries using Azzopardi et al.'s method is quite small. For example, to generate 100,000 6-word queries for WT10g takes only about **266 sec.** on OldMac, including start-up time, with a generation rate of approximately **376 queries/sec.**

As it stands this may not be fast enough for generating live query streams. Some speed up is possible using multiple cores, despite shared memory. Using three parallel runs on OldMac achieved a combined rate of **750 queries/sec**. With more attention to coding efficiency and use of a faster processor (e.g., NewMac) the rate may be increased to well over 1000 queries/sec.

Of course the rate of generation increases with the mean length of queries to be generated and reduces with the size of the corpus. Single-threaded generation of queries on OldMac with a mean length of 3 word from the TREC-AP corpus achieved a rate of **1548 queries/sec**.

10.3.5   EVALUATION OF THE QUERY STREAM SIMULATION APPROACH

In future work an obvious experiment to evaluate the query log emulation approach would make use of the 200,000 T8 NLQs queries. They should be compatible with the WT10g corpus since they comprise queries submitted to web search engines at around the time of the WT10g crawl. We could use QUERYLOGEMULATOR to convert them to queries suitable for an emulated version of WT10g and measure the rate of emulation.

Then we could run both the real query log against the real corpus and the emulated log against the emulated corpus. If the query log emulation method is successful there should be similar numbers of matches to corresponding queries in the real and emulated logs, and similar overall processing times.

Finally, we could use the query log emulator to produce a log applicable to TREC-all. Running the emulated query log should result in more matches and slower query processing than if we ran the T8 NLQs queries against TREC-all.

CHAPTER 11

Leaking Confidential Information

In discussion of collection emulation thus far we have focused on achieving fidelity of emulation, and shown that achieving high fidelity requires complex models with many parameters.

A trade-off which we now examine is the increasing exposure of confidential information occasioned by increasing fidelity of emulation. The most faithful emulation would be an exact copy but this would entail complete loss of privacy. Less faithful emulations also cause leakage of information but to a lesser degree.

Note that if we are not operating in the private data scenario the fact that an emulation method potentially leaks information is of no concern. In this case a researcher may choose the best applicable emulation method regardless of information leakage.

How can we quantify the leakage occasioned by an emulation method? How can we represent the trade-off between fidelity and privacy leakage in such a way that the custodian of a private corpus can choose an emulation method which achieves useful fidelity while limiting the risk of damage due to leakage of confidential information? Let us briefly look at the field of Information Privacy.

A large amount of research into information privacy has focused on databases containing information about individuals—how can aggregate information be extracted from databases without risking harm to the individuals whose data they contain? One form of privacy attack involves taking differences between answer sets for aggregate queries. How many people have coronavirus? How many people who aren't named X have coronavirus? The difference between precise answers to those two questions tells us whether X has coronavirus or not.

Differential privacy (e.g., [33]) essentially guarantees that even if an adversary has information about all but one person in a data set they still cannot deduce the information about the last person. The means of achieving this is essentially by adding noise—answers to aggregate queries must always include some random noise.

The case of an emulated document corpus doesn't fit the differential privacy pattern—the adversaries (i.e., the information retrieval researchers and engineers) have full access to the emulated corpus. Furthermore the information in need of protection is usually not at all like the information in a medical database. It isn't usually characterized by simple facts about individuals. Examples of information which may be considered confidential include:

- arguments to be used by the legal team in forthcoming litigation;

- indications of which chemicals are currently being studied by the research department;

- specifications of a new product and its release date;

- the dollar value of a forthcoming bid for a government tender;

- romantic emails between company employees;

- plans for a forthcoming military attack; and

- documentation of when the company first knew that its main product was carcinogenic.

Extracting information such as this relates more to the field of cryptanalysis than to information privacy. There are many texts on cryptanalysis, for example [82], which cover methods for re-creating plaintext from an enciphered version.

In earlier chapters we discussed the use of substitution ciphers, pointing out that letter substitution ciphers such as Caesar1 are easily broken by using letter frequency analysis. It is clear that word substitution ciphers such as Nomenclator would be much harder to break by frequency analysis. In the latter case, letter frequency analysis achieves nothing. Word frequency analysis may reveal the identity of commonly occurring words such as "the," "and," and "of" but rare words conveying the most confidential information are unlikely to be decrypted using this approach. Once common words are decrypted it may be possible to use n-gram frequencies to decode others.

We inserted some fake confidential information (names of people involved in an office liaison, and the release date of a product) into a corpus of 50,000 TREC documents, then encrypted the corpus with Nomenclator and challenged colleagues to extract the confidential information. Nobody took up the challenge!

A defense against decryption of common words would be to assign multiple alternate cipher words to each common plain word, but this would reduce the fidelity of emulation.

A potential point of weakness for the Nomenclator method is the mapping between plain and cipher words. If that mapping were given to an adversary then all confidentiality would be lost. In a less extreme case, part of the table may be deduced if the adversary finds a quantity of parallel text—i.e., plain text with its enciphered version. A further weakness of Nomenclator is that the sequence of words in the plain text is preserved. Once the word-to-word mappings are known the entire meaning of the text is clear.

That weakness is not present in the methods based on random sequences, i.e., the word-based Markov methods and the corpusGenerator methods. In these methods, like Nomenclator, there is a one-to-one mapping from words in $\mathbb{B}$ to words in $\mathbb{M}$ which may be partially guessed using frequency analysis. Indeed, in the case of our word-based Markov implementations, the words of the plain text appear in the cipher text and with similar frequencies. However, the disruption of normal word ordering severely restricts the reliable extraction of information, even if some words are known. For example, the presence of an interesting word like `iphone12` in a random sequence of words such as `marble it iphone12 nitro sausage` may whet but not satisfy the desire for information about the new iphone.

The disruption of natural word order is complete in the case of CORPUSGENERATOR in the absence of *n*-gram modeling. Word occurrences are put into an array, shuffled, then assigned to documents and shuffled again. Some order is re-introduced when *n*-grams are modeled. It is possible to statistically analyze $\mathbb{M}$ and identify the significant *n*-grams and their frequency of occurrence, which may allow some intelligent information guessing.

Note that emulation methods which under-generate the vocabulary of the original corpus, inherently suppress information, including confidential information. BASELINE and WB-MARKOV1 are examples of such methods. The effect is significant because it is rare, possibly information-rich, words which are mostly likely to disappear.

The conditional probabilities built into higher-order word-based Markov methods which use the vocabulary of $\mathbb{B}$ may yield significant information. For example, if the sequence `June 23 invade` occurs in $\mathbb{M}$ resulting from an unsmoothed order-2 model it implies that that sequence of words was seen at least once in $\mathbb{B}$.

If an adversary had access to the Markov generator and could run it repeatedly, much more reliable information could be obtained.

In an application where preservation of confidential information is critical, it would be advisable to use smoothing (adding random noise), and avoid high Markov orders.

11.1   A SMALL EXPERIMENT ON INFORMATION LEAKAGE

We conducted an exploratory experiment with STRINGMARKOVGEN to illustrate the potential loss of confidentiality. Figure 4.6 shows the percentage of sentences in generated corpora which also occurred in the training corpus. For high-order models, the sentence overlap for the T8 NLQs corpus exceeds 90%. If T8 NLQs were a confidential corpus, emulation by this method would result in disastrous loss of confidentiality. Figure 4.7 shows that the sentence overlap reduces substantially as the level of noise increases.

The sentence overlap shown in Figure 4.6 for TREC-AP is much smaller than for T8 NLQs but, as noted in Section 4.5.1, for $k = 23$, 2184 sentences from $\mathbb{M}$ were quoted from $\mathbb{B}$. Addition of the highest level of noise ($\lambda = 0.1$) reduced the number of overlapping sentences to seven, of which only three were long enough to convey any significant meaning.

Possible reasons for the very different results for T8 NLQs and TREC-AP include:

- much more extensive training data for TREC-AP,

- shorter sentences (natural language queries) for T8 NLQs, and

- lack of sophistication in sentence breaking heuristics may have affected TREC-AP more than T8 NLQs.

Sentence overlap is of limited value as a measure of information leakage, since valuable information may leak in smaller units than sentences, and since algorithmic delineation of sentences is problematic in some document types (e.g., in lists and tables).

Future work might address leakage of smaller units of information such as *n*-grams or named entities, and extend the study of overlaps to all the other applicable methods. Naturally, methods such as CAESAR1 and variants of CORPUSGENERATOR, which generate a totally different vocabulary, are unsuitable for this type of analysis but may still leak information.

11.2   LEAKAGE OF INFORMATION VIA NEURAL MODELS

It seems that the high plausibility of word sequences generated from neural models is likely to result in risk of information leakage. Countering this in the case of GPT-2 is that one starts with a generic model trained on huge volumes of text and fine-tunes it on $\mathbb{B}$.

In the following examples we illustrate the behavior of the generic GPT-2 model. The text in boldface is the start of a possible next paragraph of this chapter. We pasted it in to "Talk to Transformer"[1] and asked it to generate three alternative completions. The output in each case is shown in italics.

Our understanding of neural methods such as GPT-2 and the properties of the text they generate is quite limited *(although it appears that that will improve). – In practice, computing the text for a typical (three line) games are not too computationally intensive. And in this case, as we know from earlier, text length scales very much with the game . . .*

Our understanding of neural methods such as GPT-2 and the properties of the text they generate is quite limited *but we may start to solve some of those puzzles by reverse-engineering the Golgi apparatus which plays such a key role. . . .*

Our understanding of neural methods such as GPT-2 and the properties of the text they generate is quite limited *and empirically it is found that GPT-2 can recognize simpler tokens (e.g., fast and long characters) as well as non-deterministic (unpredictable) tokens (e.g., string, valid and invalid) when they are placed on a basic palette . . .*

Although the generated completions appear to make no semantic sense, it is clear that "Talk to Transformer" has a very good model of linguistic sequences in the text on which it was trained. We suspect that if the model were trained only on the data in $\mathbb{B}$ that the resulting $\mathbb{M}$ would leak substantial information, even if only in the form of probabilities rather than facts. The approach we took in using a generically trained model and fine-tuning it on $\mathbb{B}$ may reduce the degree of information leakage. How the degree of leakage might vary with the amount of fine-tuning is unknown.

---

[1]https://talktotransformer.com/ accessed February 25, 2020.

Table 11.1: Rule of thumb ratings of information leakage risk for corpus emulation methods considered in this monograph

Risk of Information Leakage	Method	Available Mitigations
High	CAESAR	–
Medium	NOMENCLATOR	Map common words to multiple alternative cipher words
	High-order word-based MARKOV	Use lower order, map words
	Neural methods	Use more generic training data
	SOPHSYNTH	Don't use n-grams
Low	SIMPLESYNTH	–
	SOPHSYNTH without n-grams	–
	Low-order WBMARKOV	–

The problem of information leakage from generative machine learning systems is beginning to generate a substantial literature. A thorough review is beyond the scope of this monograph, but we mention a few articles to give a flavor. Although the paper is in the area of pharmacogenetics, Frederikson et al. [36] warn of the danger of "model inversion," i.e., the risk that a machine learned model can leak information about an original dataset. Hayes et al. [43] discuss membership inference attacks—"given a data point, the adversary determines whether or not it was used to train the model." Xu et al. [91] propose GANobfuscator, a differentially private GAN (Generative Adversarial Network), which operates by adding random noise.

Interestingly, Bellovin et al. [9] propose the use of synthetic data as another tool for preserving privacy and discuss the implications under the legal framework for privacy in the USA. The framework they discuss is solely concerned with protecting PII (Personally Identifiable Information) which doesn't match our confidentiality concern.

11.3   DISCUSSION AND CONCLUSIONS

Unfortunately, notwithstanding our exploration of sentence overlap, we currently have no widely applicable objective way to measure potential for leakage of confidential information. Table 11.1 summarizes the authors' subjective assessment of the risk of information leakage for various emulation methods discussed in the monograph. The STRINGMARKOVGEN method is not included in the table since its rating depends totally on the values of k, w, and λ.

Naturally, the decision of whether to emulate a confidential corpus and, if so, what emulation method should be used, rests entirely with the owner of the data. We hope that by presenting and analyzing a range of approaches to emulation informed decisions can be made.

For highly classified corpora, it is unlikely that emulation of any form would be permitted. Because search is important in these environments, we imagine that trusted engineers might be employed to do the tuning of search facilities on the real data.

CHAPTER 12

Discussion, Conclusions, and Future Work

There are two principal use cases for simulating information retrieval test collections:

1. emulating private corpora to train and tune algorithms, and to estimate hardware requirements; and

2. generating artificial test collections to support academic research, particularly into efficiency and scalability.

For the first use case we have explored the trade-off between fidelity of emulation and risk of leakage of confidential information. To assist data owners decide whether and how to use simulation, we have attempted to rate different emulation methods according to the risk of such leakage.

For the second use case, methods like CAESAR1 and NOMENCLATOR, whose primary purpose is to obfuscate, need not be considered. We note that the macro properties methods embodied in CORPUSGENERATOR allow researchers to distribute terabytes of simulated text data by sharing less than a kilobyte of parameters. CORPUSGENERATOR also allows researchers to carry out meaningful and reproducible studies of algorithm scalability and to engineer corpora with specific sizes and properties for systematic study of the effects of varying parameters such as vocabulary size, or the shape of the word probability distribution.

The Markov and neural methods have the potential to provide more realistic emulation of linguistic structures than has been achieved with macro properties methods. That makes them more suited to the tuning of retrieval algorithms in the private corpora scenario. However, more accurate linguistic modeling is very likely to increase leakage of confidential information. Markov and neural methods also have disadvantages in academic research scenarios:

- If there's no confidentiality concern, it may be possible to use the real corpus.

- Models are large.

- It's not clear that they can be used to realistically scale up a corpus.

After studying a number of corpora with diverse properties we have discussed a range of models for each of:

- word frequency distribution;

- word representation strings;

- document length distribution;

- letter frequency distribution;

- word length distribution;

- correlation of word frequency and word length;

- term dependence; and

- corpus growth.

12.1   SUMMARY OF METHODS INVESTIGATED

Table 12.1 summarizes in broad terms the specific corpus emulation methods we have studied in this monograph. Which of the specific methods is best suited to a particular application will depend upon which corpus characteristics are important to model faithfully, how important is it to control the risk of information leakage, whether scaling up is required, and whether rates of generation and scale of computational resources are important. Using these characteristics to filter the table may yield a small set of candidate methods. On the other hand, the requirements may be over-constrained and must be relaxed unless mitigations can be found for dimensions where requirements cannot be met. Many of the methods provide choices and options, which allow potential mitigation.

12.2   SYNTHACORPUS

We have provided a set of open source tools SYNTHACORPUS which are capable of extracting properties from a base corpus $\mathbb{B}$ and generating a simulated (mimic) corpus $\mathbb{M}$ which matches the properties and conforms to the models. SYNTHACORPUS includes tools for realistic scaling up of an existing corpus and two different methods of generating compatible query sets. It also provides implementations of other methods for generating synthetic text such as word-based and string-based Markov methods and substitution ciphers.

A principal tool in SYNTHACORPUS is the previously mentioned CORPUSGENERATOR. Its approach to generating a synthetic corpus is essentially a language-model one, though we attempt a relatively sophisticated model which takes into account some types of term dependency, and growth in vocabulary. We also prevent the under-generation of vocabulary inherent in simple language models by efficiently implementing sampling without replacement.

Pros of the CORPUSGENERATOR approach include:

- speed of generation;

Table 12.1: A broad brush summary of the specific methods for emulating a real corpus which we have studied in this monograph. Note that CORPUSGENERATOR is able to employ a wide range of generative models but we have picked three specific combinations. **Notes:** "Comp. resources" characterizes the CPU/GPU time and memory requirements for training and generation. SophSynth needs large memory for extracting n-grams. "Commun. size" refers to the minimum amount of data communicated to allow a researcher to generate the emulated corpus. "Emulation fidelity" lists the dimensions on which faithful emulation is achieved. The last column refers to the relationship between word frequency and word length.

Method		Characteristics						Emulation Fidelity							
Name	Type	Training spd	Generation spd	Risk Information Leak	Scalability	Comp. Resources	Communication Size	Vocabulary size	Word Frequencies	n-grams	Bursts	Co-occurences	Document Lengths	Word Lengths	Frequency vs. Length
CAESAR1	Cipher	N/A	Fstst	High	N/A	vSm	Lg	✓	✓	✓	✓	✓	✓	✓	✓
NOMENCLATOR	Cipher	N/A	vFst	Med	N/A	Sm	Lg	✓	✓	✓	✓	✓	✓	✓	
BASELINE	Cntxt-free LM	Fst	Fst	Low	limVoc	Sm	Lg	✓					✓	✓	
WBMARKOV0	Cntxt-free LM	Fst	Slw	Low	limVoc	Sm	Lg	✓						✓	
WBMARKOV1	Cntxt-sen. LM	Slw	Slw	Med	limVoc	Lg	vLg	✓	✓					✓	✓
STRINGMARKOV	Cntxt-sen. LM	Slw	Slw	Var	OK	Lg	vLg	✓	✓	✓				✓	✓
SIMPLESYNTH	Macro prop.s	vFst	vFst	Low	Good	Sm	Sm	✓					✓		
SOPHSYNTH	Macro prop.s	Fst	vFst	Med	Good	Lg	Med	✓	✓	✓			✓	✓	?
GPT-2	Neural	vSlw	vSlw	Med	?	vLg	vLg	✓	✓	?	?			✓	

- accuracy of modeling various aspects of words, documents and corpora;

- compact models;

- ability to realistically scale-up a corpus;

- ability to engineer a corpus with desired macro properties; and

- preservation of confidentiality, since the placement and order of words is random and the word strings may be arbitrarily changed.

Cons include:

- the resulting text is unrealistic and conveys no meaning, limiting its usefulness in many information retrieval (e.g., TREC ad hoc task) or NLP scenarios; and

- the current implementation in SYNTHACORPUS doesn't accurately model association between terms, particularly co-occurrence and burstiness.

Hardware needed: Our work on this project initially focused on extremely large corpora and machines with terabytes of RAM. To make the work more accessible and reproducible we changed to publicly available test collections such as those of TREC, and to hardware configurations accessible to nearly all researchers. Apart from the work with GPT-2, nearly all of the experimental results presented here were obtained on Apple MacBook Pro laptops OldMac and NewMac. Timing results were obtained using OldMac, a laptop dating from early 2013, with 16 GB of RAM. The code in SYNTHACORPUS is written entirely in C11 and Perl and has very little dependence on external packages. We recommend use of a machine with at least 16 GB of RAM.

Unfortunately, although it is possible to run GPT-2 on a laptop like NewMac, exploration of the exciting potential of neural text generators is likely to benefit from much more expensive hardware such as arrays of GPUs.

12.3   TOWARD MORE NATURAL LANGUAGE

Although GPT-2 generates superficially plausible text, the result has no meaning. This means that it can't be used to support queries whose evaluation relies on advanced linguistic constructs. For example, "trials by legislatures of ginger-haired political officials who live in light-colored houses."

In the future it may be possible to more explicitly model the process of creating documents and their text. Considering the Associated Press collection, each article would be generated by an author, possibly commissioned by an editor, and edited by a sub-editor. The author would start with an event and a set of related facts. They would have in mind a target length. They would write a story starting with a heading and then a summary first paragraph, and comprising prose written according to the Associated Press style. The editor might have specified the target length and drawn attention to the event. The sub-editor might change the heading, correct spelling errors, edit the text, and trim the article to length.

Simulating this might start by randomly generating events and pseudo-facts around them. Some attempts have been made by others to automatically generate text from this type of starting point. These are discussed in Section 1.6.4. One could generate a sports corpus by repeatedly generating sportscasts—each time generating facts by picking two cities, choosing animal or other names for their teams, then inventing facts, score lines, and player actions.

This more sophisticated approach would generate more believable text but it wouldn't be as useful for the task of enabling efficiency and other measurements on emulated versions of private corpora.

12.4   FUTURE WORK

We have tried to make this work comprehensive but there are a number of areas where substantial future work is needed.

1. The modeling of compound terms in CORPUSGENERATOR is far from the final word. We haven't properly solved the problem of overlapping n-grams and we haven't implemented other forms of term association such as burstiness and co-occurrence. There is opportunity here both for theoretical development and practical implementation.

2. There is scope for further exploration of methods capable of generating more linguistically realistic text, particularly neural methods.

3. Our small exploration of sentence overlap between $\mathbb{M}$ and $\mathbb{B}$ has barely scratched the surface of the problem of quantifying the risk of leakage of confidential information.

4. Quite a number of smaller future work items are listed in individual chapters.

We offer SYNTHACORPUS to both the academic research and commercial communities and hope that others will use it and contribute improvements. The first release of SYNTHACORPUS was developed while the first author was employed by Microsoft. He gratefully acknowledges Microsoft's willingness to open source the code, thereby allowing him to share it with the community, to continue to work on it in his retirement, and to prepare this monograph.

Bibliography

[1] Nima Asadi, Donald Metzler, Tamer Elsayed, and Jimmy Lin. Pseudo test collections for learning Web search ranking functions. In *Proc. of SIGIR*, pages 1073–1082, 2011. DOI: 10.1145/2009916.2010058 112

[2] Leif Azzopardi. The economics in interactive information retrieval. In *Proc. of SIGIR*, pages 15–24, 2011. DOI: 10.1145/2009916.2009923 5

[3] Leif Azzopardi and Maarten de Rijke. Automatic construction of known-item finding test beds. In *Proc. of SIGIR*, pages 603–604, 2006. DOI: 10.1145/1148170.1148276 4, 112

[4] Leif Azzopardi, Maarten de Rijke, and Krisztian Balog. Building simulated queries for known-item topics: An analysis using six European languages. In *Proc. of SIGIR*, pages 455–462, 2007. DOI: 10.1145/1277741.1277820 4, 112, 113

[5] Ricardo Baeza-Yates. Incremental sampling of query logs. In *Proc. of SIGIR*, pages 1093–1096, 2015. DOI: 10.1145/2766462.2776780 35

[6] Ricardo Baeza-Yates and Gonzalo Navarro. Modeling text databases. In Ricardo Baeza-Yates, Joseph Glaz, Henryk Gzyl, Jürgen Hüsler, and José Luis Palacios, Eds., *Recent Advances in Applied Probability*, pages 1–25. Springer, Boston, MA, 2005. DOI: 10.1007/0-387-23394-6_1 4, 28, 35, 49, 94, 111, 119

[7] Norman R. Baker and Richard E. Nance. The use of simulation in studying information storage and retrieval systems. *JASIST*, 19(4):363–370, October 1968. DOI: 10.1002/asi.5090190402 4

[8] Timothy C. Bell, John G. Cleary, and Ian H. Witten. *Text Compression*. Prentice Hall, Upper Saddle River, NJ, 1990. 6

[9] Steven M. Bellovin, Preetam K. Dutta, and Nathan Reitinger. Privacy and synthetic datasets. *Stanford Technology Law Review*, 22(1), 2019. DOI: 10.2139/ssrn.3255766 145

[10] Richard Berendsen, Manos Tsagkias, Maarten de Rijke, and Edgar Meij. Generating pseudo test collections for learning to rank scientific articles. In *Information Access Evaluation. Multilinguality, Multimodality, and Visual Analytics*, volume LNCS 7488 of *Lecture Notes in Computer Science*, pages 42–53, Springer Berlin Heidelberg, 2012. DOI: 10.1007/978-3-642-33247-0_6 112

[11] Richard Berendsen, Manos Tsagkias, Wouter Weerkamp, and Maarten de Rijke. Pseudo test collections for training and tuning microblog rankers. In *Proc. of SIGIR*, pages 53–62, 2013. DOI: 10.1145/2484028.2484063 112

[12] Bodo Billerbeck, Justin Zobel, Nicholas Lester, and Nick Craswell. Scalable Methods for Calculating Term Co-Occurrence Frequencies. *arXiv e-prints*, page arXiv:2007.08709, July 2020. 48, 57

[13] David M. Blei, Andrew Y. Ng, and Michael I. Jordan. Latent Dirichlet allocation. *The Journal of Machine Learning Research*, 3:993–1022, 2003. 12

[14] Charles R. Blunt, Robert T. Duquet, and Peter T. Luckie. A general model for simulating information storage and retrieval systems. Information Systems Branch, Office of Naval Research, April 1966. http://www.dtic.mil/dtic/tr/fulltext/u2/636435.pdf DOI: 10.21236/ad0636435 4

[15] Pia Borlund and Jesper W. Schneider. Reconsideration of the simulated work task situation: A context instrument for evaluation of information retrieval interaction. In *Proc. of IIiX*, pages 155–164, 2010. DOI: 10.1145/1840784.1840808 5

[16] C. P. Bourne and D. F. Ford. Cost analysis and simulation procedures for evaluation of large information systems. *American Documentation*, April 1964. 4

[17] Fidel Cacheda, Victor Carneiro, Vassilis Plachouras, and Iadh Ounis. Performance analysis of distributed information retrieval architectures using an improved network simulation model. *Information Processing and Management*, 43(1):204–224, January 2007. DOI: 10.1016/j.ipm.2006.06.002 4

[18] Brendon Cahoon and Kathryn S. McKinley. Performance evaluation of a distributed architecture for information retrieval. In *Proc. of SIGIR*, pages 110–118, 1996. DOI: 10.1145/243199.243238 4

[19] David L. Chen, Joohyun Kim, and Raymond J. Mooney. Training a multilingual sportscaster: Using perceptual context to learn language. *Journal of Artificial Intelligence Research*, 37:397–435, 2010. DOI: 10.1613/jair.2962 14

[20] Mia Xu Chen, Benjamin N. Lee, Gagan Bansal, Yuan Cao, Shuyuan Zhang, Justin Lu, Jackie Tsay, Yinan Wang, Andrew M. Dai, Zhifeng Chen, Timothy Sohn, and Yonghui Wu. Gmail smart compose: Real-time assisted writing. In *Proc. of KDD*, August 2019. DOI: 10.1145/3292500.3330723 14

[21] Stanley F. Chen and Joshua Goodman. An empirical study of smoothing techniques for language modeling. In *Proc. of the 34th Annual Meeting of the ACL*, 1996. https://arxiv.org/pdf/cmp-lg/9606011.pdf DOI: 10.3115/981863.981904 13

[22] Ed H. Chi, Peter Pirolli, Kim Chen, and James Pitkow. Using information scent to model user information needs and actions and the web. In *Proc. of CHI*, pages 490–497, 2001. DOI: 10.1145/365024.365325 5

[23] Flavio Chierichetti, Ravi Kumar, and Bo Pang. On the power laws of language: Word frequency distributions. In *Proc. of SIGIR*, pages 385–394, ACM, New York, 2017. DOI: 10.1145/3077136.3080821 35

[24] Charles Clarke, Nick Craswell, and Ian Soboroff. Overview of the TREC 2004 Terabyte Track. In *Proc. of TREC*, NIST, 2004. 15

[25] Michael D. Cooper. A simulation model of a retrieval system. *Information Storage and Retrieval*, 9:13–32, 1973. http://beachmat.berkeley.edu/mike/Articles/IPMSimulation1973.pdf 3

[26] Nick Craswell, Daniel Campos, Bhaskar Mitra, Emine Yilmaz, and Bodo Billerbeck. ORCAS: 18 million clicked query-document pairs for analyzing search, 2020. https://arxiv.org/abs/2006.05324 117

[27] Nick Craswell, David Hawking, and Kathleen Griffiths. Which search engine is best at finding airline site home pages? Technical Report 01/45, CSIRO Mathematical and Information Sciences, 2001. http://david-hawking.net/pubs/craswell_tr01.pdf 111

[28] W. Bruce Croft, Stephen Harding, Kazem Taghva, and Julie Borsack. An evaluation of information retrieval accuracy with simulated OCR output. In *Symposium of Document Analysis and Information Retrieval*, 1994. https://ciir-publications.cs.umass.edu/pub/web/getpdf.php?id=109 5

[29] Van Dang and W. Bruce Croft. Query reformulation using anchor text. In *Proc. of WSDM*, ACM, New York, 2010. DOI: 10.1145/1718487.1718493 111

[30] Marie Laure Delignette-Muller and Christophe Dutang. fitdistrplus: An R package for fitting distributions. *Journal of Statistical Software*, 64(4):1–34, 2015. DOI: 10.18637/jss.v064.i04 28

[31] Shuai Ding, Josh Attenberg, and Torsten Suel. Scalable techniques for document identifier assignment in inverted indexes. In *Proc. of WWW*, pages 311–320, 2010. DOI: 10.1145/1772690.1772723 15

[32] Richard Durstenfeld. Algorithm 235: Random permutation. *Communications of the ACM*, 7(7):420–421, July 1964. DOI: 10.1145/364520.364540 30

[33] Cynthia Dwork and Aaron Roth. *The Algorithmic Foundations of Differential Privacy*, vol. 9 of *Foundations and Trends in Theoretical Computer Science*. NOW Publishers, Hanover MA, 2014. 141

[34] Leo Egghe. Untangling Herdan's law and Heaps' law: Mathematical and infometric arguments. *JASIST*, 58(5):702–709, 2007. DOI: 10.1002/asi.20524 5

[35] Colum Foley and Alan F. Smeaton. Synchronous collaborative information retrieval: Techniques and evaluation. In *Proc. of ECIR*, pages 42–53, 2009. DOI: 10.1007/978-3-642-00958-7_7 5

[36] Matthew Fredrikson, Eric Lantz, Somesh Jha, Simon Lin, David Page, and Thomas RistenPart. Privacy in pharmacogenetics: An end-to-end case study of personalized warfarin dosing. In *Proc. of the 23rd USENIX Security Symposium*, 2014. 145

[37] J. B. Fried, et al. Index simulation feasibility and automatic document classification. Technical Report: Computer and Information Science Research Center, Ohio State University, 1968. CFSTI Report BP182597. 4

[38] Paul A. Gagniuc. *Markov Chains: From Theory to Implementation and Experimentation.* Wiley, 2017. DOI: 10.1002/9781119387596 70

[39] Michael D. Gordon. Evaluating the effectiveness of information retrieval systems using simulated queries. *Journal of the American Society for Information Science*, 41(5):313–323, 1990. DOI: 10.1002/(sici)1097-4571(199007)41:5<313::aid-asi1>3.0.co;2-g 3

[40] J. M. Griffiths. The computer simulation of information retrieval experiments. Ph.D. thesis, University College London, 1978. 3

[41] David Hawking, Nick Craswell, Francis Crimmins, and Trystan Upstill. How valuable is external link evidence when searching enterprise webs? In *Proc. of the Australasian Database Conference (ADC)*, pages 77–84, January 2004. http://david-hawking.net/pubs/hawking_adc04.pdf 111

[42] David Hawking, Nick Craswell, and Paul Thistlewaite. Overview of TREC-7 very large collection track. In *Proc. of TREC-7*, pages 91–104, November 1998. NIST special publication 500-242, http://trec.nist.gov/pubs/trec7/t7_proceedings.html 108

[43] Jamie Hayes, Luca Melis, George Danezis, and Emiliano de Cristofaro. LOGAN: Membership inference attacks against generative models. In *Proc. of Privacy Enhancing Technologies Symposium*, July 2019. https://arxiv.org/pdf/1705.07663.pdf DOI: 10.2478/popets-2019-0008 145

[44] R. M. Hayes and Kevin D. Reilly. The effect of response time upon utilization of an information storage and retrieval system—a simulation. In *Proc. of Annual Meeting of the Operations Research Society of America*, June 1967. http://files.eric.ed.gov/fulltext/ED033732.pdf 4

[45] Harold Stanley Heaps. *Information Retrieval: Computational and Theoretical Aspects*, Chapter 7.5, pages 206–208. Academic Press, 1978. 5, 10

[46] Michael D. Heine. Simulation, and simulation experiments. In Karen Spärck Jones, Ed., *Information Retrieval Experiment*, Butterworth and Co., London, 1981. https://sigir.org/files/museum/Information_Retrieval_Experiment/pdfs/p179-heine.pdf. 4

[47] Steffen Heinz, Justin Zobel, and Hugh E. Williams. Burst tries: A fast, efficient data structure for string keys. *ACM Transactions on Information Systems*, 20(2):192–223, 2002. DOI: 10.1145/506309.506312 84

[48] Gustav Herdan. *Type-Token Mathematics: A Textbook of Mathematical Linguistics*. Mouton, The Hague, 1960. 5, 10

[49] Sepp Hochreiter and Jürgen Schmidhuber. Long short-term memory. *Neural Computation*, 9(8):1735–1780, 1997. DOI: 10.1162/neco.1997.9.8.1735 70

[50] Bouke Huurnink, Katja Hofmann, Maarten De Rijke, and Marc Bron. Validating query simulators: An experiment using commercial searches and purchases. In *Proc. of CLEF*, pages 40–51, Springer-Verlag, Berlin, Heidelberg, 2010. DOI: 10.1007/978-3-642-15998-5_6 112

[51] Kalervo Jävelin and Jaana Kekäläinen. Cumulative gain-based evaluation of IR techniques. *ACM Transactions on Information Systems*, 20(4):422–446, October 2002. DOI: 10.1145/582415.582418 1

[52] Tapas Kanungo. Document degradation models and a methodology for degradation model validation. Ph.D. thesis, University of Washington, 1996. http://www.kanungo.com/pubs/phdthesis.pdf 5

[53] Jinyoung Kim and W. Bruce Croft. Retrieval experiments using pseudo-desktop collections. In *Proc. of CIKM*, 2009. DOI: 10.1145/1645953.1646117 5, 112

[54] Roberto Konow, Gonzalo Navarro, Charles L. A. Clarke, and Alejandro López-Ortíz. Faster and smaller inverted indices with treaps. In *Proc. of SIGIR*, pages 193–202, 2013. DOI: 10.1145/2484028.2484088 15

[55] Ioannis Konstas and Mirella Lapata. Concept-to-text generation via discriminative reranking. In *Proc. of ACL*, pages 369–378, 2012. https://www.aclweb.org/anthology/P12-1039.pdf 14

[56] Dominique Labbé. Experiments on authorship attribution by intertextual distance in English. *Journal of Quantitative Linguistics*, 14, April 2007. DOI: 10.1080/09296170600850601 132

[57] Jean Laherrère. Distributions de type "fractal parabolique" dans la nature. *Comptes Rendus de l'Académie des Sciences. Série 2a, Sciences de la Terre et des Planètes*, 322:535–541, 1996. In French with English summary. 35

[58] Gerard Ledger. An exploration of differences in the Pauline Epistles using multivariate statistical analysis. *Literary and Linguistic Computing*, 10(2):85–97, January 1995. DOI: 10.1093/llc/10.2.85 132

[59] G. Marsaglia and T. A. Bray. A convenient method for generating normal variables. *SIAM Review*, 6:260–264, 1964. DOI: 10.1137/1006063 27

[60] George Marsaglia and Wai Wan Tsang. A simple method for generating gamma variables. *ACM Transactions on Mathematical Software*, 26(3):363–372, 2000. DOI: 10.1145/358407.358414 27

[61] Makoto Matsumoto and Takuji Nishimura. Mersenne Twister: A 623-dimensionally equidistributed uniform pseudo-random number generator. *ACM Transactions on Modeling and Computer Simulation*, 8(1):3–30, 1998. DOI: 10.1145/272991.272995 33, 38

[62] David Maxwell. Modelling Search and Stopping in Interactive Information Retrieval. Ph.D. thesis, School of Computing Science, University of Glasgow, Scotland, April 2019. DOI: 10.5525/gla.thesis.41132 5

[63] G. A. Miller. Some effects of intermittent silence. *American Journal of Psychology*, 70:311–313, 1957. DOI: 10.2307/1419346 34, 94

[64] T. Minka, J. M. Winn, J. P. Guiver, S. Webster, Y. Zaykov, B. Yangel, A. Spengler, and J. Bronskill. Infer.NET 2.6, 2014. Microsoft Research Cambridge. http://research.microsoft.com/infernet 27

[65] Thomas P. Minka. Estimating a gamma distribution, 2002. http://research.microsoft.com/en-us/um/people/minka/papers/minka-gamma.pdf 27

[66] Landon Curt Noll. FNV hash. http://www.isthe.com/chongo/tech/comp/fnv/, 2020. 86

[67] OpenAI. Better language models and their implications. https://openai.com/blog/better-language-models/, February 2019. 13

[68] Casper Petersen, Jakob Grue Simonsen, and Christina Lioma. Power law distributions in information retrieval. *TOIS*, 34(2):8:1–8:37, February 2016. DOI: 10.1145/2816815 35

[69] Alec Radford, Jeffrey Wu, Rewon Child, David Luan, Dario Amodei, and Ilya Sutskever. Learning models are unsupervised multitask learners. Technical report, OpenAI, San Francisco, CA, February 2019. 13

[70] Kevin D. Reilly. Outline for a simulation study of the California state library network. Technical report, Institute of Library Research. University of California at Los Angeles, July 1968. http://files.eric.ed.gov/fulltext/ED031280.pdf 4

[71] Kevin D. Reilly. User determination of library request presentation: A simulation. Technical report, Institute of Library Research. University of California at Los Angeles, July 1968. http://files.eric.ed.gov/fulltext/ED031280.pdf 4

[72] Ehud Reiter and Robert Dale. Building applied natural language generation systems. *Natural Language Engineering*, 3(1):57–87, 1997. DOI: 10.1017/s1351324997001502 14

[73] Ehud Reiter and Robert Dale. *Building Natural Language Generation Systems*. Cambridge University Press, 2000. DOI: 10.1017/cbo9780511519857 14

[74] S. E. Robertson, S. Walker, M. M. Hancock-Beaulieu, and M. Gatford. Okapi at TREC-3. In *Proc. of TREC-3*, pages 109–126, November 1994. NIST special publication 500-225. 25

[75] Stephen Robertson, Evangelos Kanoulas, and Emine Yilmaz. Modelling score distributions without actual scores. In *Proc. of ICTIR*, pages 85–92, Association for Computing Machinery, New York, 2013. DOI: 10.1145/2499178.2499181 5

[76] Thomas Aneirin Rowlands. Information retrieval through textual annotations. Ph.D. thesis, Australian National University, 2012. https://openresearch-repository.anu.edu.au/handle/1885/149606 112

[77] Mark Sanderson. *Test Collection Based Evaluation of Information Retrieval Systems*, vol. 4. Foundations and Trends in Information Retrieval, 2010. DOI: 10.1561/1500000009 1

[78] Jacques Savoy. *Machine Learning Methods for Stylometry. Authorship Atribution and Author Profiling*. Springer, 2020. DOI: 10.1007/978-3-030-53360-1 132

[79] Claude Shannon. A mathematical theory of communication. *The Bell System Technical Journal*, 27:379–423, 1948. DOI: 10.1002/j.1538-7305.1948.tb01338.x 69, 70

[80] Bengt Sigurd, Mats Eeg-Olofsson, and Joost van der Weijer. Word length, sentence length and frequency—Zipf revisited. *Studia Linguistica*, 58(1):37–52, 2004. DOI: 10.1111/j.0039-3193.2004.00109.x 65, 68

[81] Amit Singhal, Gerard Salton, Mandar Mitra, and Chris Buckley. Document length normalization. Technical Report TR95-1529, Department of Computer Science, Cornell University, Ithaca NY, 1995. 25

[82] Mark Stamp and Richard M. Low. *Applied Cryptanalysis: Breaking Ciphers in the Real World*, 1st ed., Wiley-IEEE Press, 2007. 142

[83] Ilya Sutskever, James Martens, and Geoffrey E. Hinton. Generating text with recurrent neural networks. In *Proc. of ICML*, pages 1017–1024, 2011. 13, 69, 70

[84] Jean Tague, Michael Nelson, and Harry Wu. Problems in the simulation of bibliographic retrieval systems. In *Proc. of SIGIR*, pages 236–255, Butterworth and Co, Kent, UK, 1981. 3

[85] C. J. van Rijsbergen. A theoretical basis for the use of co-occurrence data in information retrieval. *Journal of Documentation*, 33(2):106–119, 1977. DOI: 10.1108/eb026637 3

[86] Ashish Vaswani, Noam Shazeer, Niki Parmar, Jakob Uszkoreit, Llion Jones, Aidan N. Gomez, Lukasz Kaiser, and Illi Polosukhin. Attention is all you need. In *Proc. of NIPS)*, 2017. https://papers.nips.cc/paper/7181-attention-is-all-you-need.pdf 13

[87] Ellen M. Voorhees and Donna K. Harman. *TREC: Experiment and Evaluation in Information Retrieval (Digital Libraries and Electronic Publishing)*. The MIT Press, 2005. 1, 16

[88] Hanna M. Wallach, Iain Murray, Ruslan Salakhutdinov, and David Mimno. Evaluation methods for topic models. In *Proc. of ICML*, pages 1105–1112, ACM, 2009. DOI: 10.1145/1553374.1553515 12

[89] William Webber and Alistair Moffat. In search of reliable retrieval experiments. In *Proc. of the Australasian Document Computing Symposium (ADCS)*, 2005. https://people. eng.unimelb.edu.au/ammoffat/abstracts/wm05adcs.pdf 4, 115

[90] Hugh E. Williams and Justin Zobel. Searchable words on the Web. *International Journal on Digital Libraries*, 5(2):99–105, 2005. DOI: 10.1007/s00799-003-0050-z 10

[91] Chugui Xu, Ju Ren, Deyu Zhang, Yaoxue Zhang, Zhan Qin, and Kui Ren. GANobfuscator: Mitigating information leakage under GAN via differential privacy. *IEEE Transactions on Information Forensics and Security*, 14(9):2358–2371, September 2019. DOI: 10.1109/tifs.2019.2897874 145

[92] George Kingsley Zipf. *The Psycho-Biology of Language*. Houghton Mifflin, Oxford, 1935. DOI: 10.4324/9781315009421 12, 65

[93] George Kingsley Zipf. *Human Behavior and the Principle of Least Effort*. Addison-Wesley, 1949. 34

[94] Justin Zobel and Alistair Moffat. Inverted files for text search engines. *ACM Computing Surveys*, 38(2), 2006. DOI: 10.1145/1132956.1132959 15

[95] Justin Zobel, Alistair Moffat, and Kotagiri Ramamohanarao. Inverted files versus signature files for text indexing. *ACM Transactions on Database Systems*, 23(4):453–490, December 1998. DOI: 10.1145/296854.277632 3, 8, 27

Authors' Biographies

DAVID HAWKING

David Hawking is an Honorary Professor in the College of Engineering and Computer Science at the Australian National University in Canberra. His research in Information Retrieval began in the early nineteen-nineties at the Australian National University where he worked on parallel and distributed IR, and proximity models of retrieval. With ANU colleagues, he coordinated the Very Large Collection and Web tracks at TREC and co-created a number of test collections, notably WT10g and VLC2. Between 1998 and 2008 he worked for the government research organisation CSIRO and, with colleagues, developed an internet and enterprise retrieval system which was spun off as Funnelback Pty Ltd. David worked as Chief Scientist for Funnelback until 2013 when he joined Microsoft and worked on the Bing search engine. He retired from paid work in 2018.

BODO BILLERBECK

Bodo Billerbeck is an applied data scientist at Microsoft Bing, working mostly on core search problems. His interests lie in finding often data-driven solutions to multiple problems in the search stack, including indexing, query reformulation, matching, answer selection and insertion, as well as evaluation. Since completing his Ph.D. at RMIT University in 2005 he briefly worked at Sensis.com.au, but soon moved on to Microsoft. After spending some time embedded at Microsoft Research in Cambridge, UK, he returned to Australia, and recently has come full circle and is enjoying an honorary fellow position at RMIT.

PAUL THOMAS

Paul Thomas is an applied scientist at Microsoft. His research is in information retrieval: particularly in how people use web search systems and how we should evaluate these systems, as well as interfaces for search including search with different types of results, search on mobile devices, and search as conversation. He has previously worked at Australia's CSIRO and the Australian National University.

NICK CRASWELL

Nick Craswell is a research manager at Microsoft Bing. Since obtaining his Ph.D. from the Australian National University in 2000 on the topic of distributed information retrieval, Nick has worked on enterprise search, expert search, anchor text, click graphs, image search, offline and online evaluation of Web search, query-independent evidence in ranking, evaluation metrics and web ranking and neural ranking models. He has been a driving force in the TREC web tracks and enterprise tracks and was instrumental in creating various widely used test collections.